Praise for *When Scars Become Stories*

Every ounce of *When Scars Become Stories* is truly anchored in hope—hope in Jesus, our Saviour and Redeemer. From the very beginning, the way Pat writes is beautiful – raw and tender, insightful and loving. I can hear her tone in each page and her approach is kind and caring, offering a safety for people in their pain yet a reminder that this is not the finish line. As I read the Forward, I immediately thought of people I wanted to get this book in front of – people who could share in the vulnerability and the tender, raw experiences of the grief she speaks of.

This book gives language to aspects of grief that many people struggle to articulate. Expressions such as "when Melanie ran ahead to heaven" gently direct the reader's attention to a greater reality beyond earthly pain. Again and again, the writing draws the heart back toward hope. Pat offers insights that create space to grieve while also providing practical steps and applications that actively support healing.

The accessible writing style makes it easy to return to, even in small moments—there is always gold to be found in its pages. Pat's thoughtful acknowledgment of both the emotional and physiological realities of grief form a strong foundation for a healing journey, offering validation and reflection while remaining firmly anchored in truth and hope.

~*Jo Watson, Pastoral Director, Passion City Church, Trilith*

When Scars Become *Stories* by Pat Elsberry is a compassionate and faith-filled guide for anyone navigating the heartbreak of child loss. Drawing from her own experience after the death of her daughter Melanie, Pat offers gentle reflections, Scripture, and prayers that bring comfort and perspective to those walking through grief.

What makes this book especially helpful for grieving parents is the way it combines Scripture, personal reflection, and gentle guidance in short, accessible chapters. Each section begins with a story or metaphor that captures what grief feels like—like "Navigating the Ocean of Grief," where she compares loss to unpredictable tides, or "The Slow-Motion Nightmare," which perfectly expresses how surreal those early days of loss can be.

Every chapter closes with a short prayer and reflection, inviting the reader to pause and meet God in the midst of pain. That rhythm makes the book ideal for those whose attention spans feel short in grief—offering comfort in small, digestible pieces.

With authenticity and biblical hope, Pat reminds readers that grief is not something to "move on" from, but a sacred journey where God's presence brings healing over time. This book helps grieving parents see that while wounds may remain, God can transform them into testimonies of endurance, faith, and love that never ends.

~Jill Sullivan, Executive Director, While We're Waiting

You are holding in your hands the words not only of my friend who has God-given authority to speak on *When Scars Become Stories*, but also the words of our God, whose authority we rest in. Pat Elsberry walks alongside the sorrowful reader with grace, gently relieving guilt and shame with an encouraging and timely word—chapter by chapter—for all who are grieving. Every hope-filled truth she shares is supported by God Himself through His word. Powerful! I first met Pat when she spoke at a ladies' event I attended. Her words were carefully chosen, captivating, and filled with grace. I left, encouraged and amazed, by the spiritual and scriptural depth of this dear lady. It was clear that God had done a refining work in her heart. Even though Pat has experienced significant loss through the death of her daughter, which she humbly shares, her life declares the glory of God. Her scars stand as a trophy of God's grace. Pat offers a lifeline of hope, reminding us that even in the darkest valleys, we have a Savior who, being acquainted with our grief, leads us through the broken places and heals our wounded souls. I highly recommend *When Scars Become Stories* for anyone with a grieving heart.

~Toni Hebel, Executive Director, ReGenerating Life Ministries
Co-Author of *Forgiving Forward*

A beautifully written testimony of God's comfort in our deepest sorrow. This book reminds us that even in loss His presence is near and His promises remain true. I love how Pat shares such honest pain and unshakable faith. This book is a beacon of hope for anyone walking through the valley of loss and reminds us that we are not alone.

~ Cheryl Juaire, President/Founder of the National Grief
Organization, Team Sharing

When Scars Become Stories is a treasure for the grieving and a guide-book for those walking alongside them. Pat's writing has touched something very deep inside me. She gives words to what I have felt and experienced personally, but never had the words to express. She has a gift for reaching into a heart with her words and sparking hope inside. I appreciate how Pat openly addresses every aspect of grief. She grants permission to feel what you feel and accept the new you that emerges. The scriptures are woven throughout the book, bringing insight and healing from God's word. Pat has given me the freedom to embrace the gift of grieving. I have found that there is purpose in pain, and this book has validated this belief.

~Martha Wilson, Founder/Executive Director,
Touching Hearts Ministries

Just as the poet Vergil guided Dante through the darkest realms of Hades, author Pat Elsberry takes our hand and guides us through the trackless valleys and over the storm-tossed seas of personal bereavement. Pat's prayerful, gentle advice, and her bravely shared stories born of deep wounds from the tragic loss of her adult daughter, bring us comfort in our distress and courage to keep going.

It has been nearly six years since I lost my spouse, and thanks to Pat Elsberry I have found a renewed perspective and a spiritual, hopeful outlook for the rest of my own earthly journey.

~Tom Burke, Author, *Evil Must Not Have the Last Word*

Pat walks alongside us, the broken hearted, grieving sojourners, as a compassionate friend. In her newest book, *When Scars Become Stories,* she peels back the curtain to reveal the reality of grief, and the sure hope of God's restoring presence. Her words became personal prayers in my own journey of grief. As I read, I felt as though I were talking with a friend over coffee, yet challenged to stay close to the God of Hope and Purpose. To echo her words as my own desire: *"I want my scars to shape me into a person marked by resilience, empathy, and grace."*

~Kim Stanley, One Thing Worship

When Scars
Become Stories

When Scars
Become Stories

*A Journey of Healing,
Restoration & Faith*

Pat Elsberry

PAT ELSBERRY PUBLISHING
Altlana, Georgia

Book Design: Mary M. Meade
Author Photo: Tamara Dixon

Pat Elsberry Publishing
First Edition
ISBN (print) 979-8-9948355-0-0
ISBN (eBook) 979-8-9948355-1-7

To my dear husband Fred, God has used your
steadfast love to lift me in the valleys.
You've seen every scar and loved me with a steady,
enduring tenderness. Thank you for walking this journey
by my side. My heart is forever grateful..

To my precious ones—John, Cameron, and my
forever girl, Melanie. Your lives have given me strength for
the journey, and your love has carried me further
than you will ever know. I will love you beyond
all my days.

Contents

PART SIX

Community and Compassion

PART SEVEN

Hope Rising in the Storm

Preface

To THE PERSON WHOSE HEART has been shattered by loss, I see you. I acknowledge your pain, your sorrow, and the weight you carry every single day. Losing someone you love changes you in ways you never imagined. In my own experience of losing my daughter, Melanie, I learned that there is no grief quite like the grief of losing a child. It's not a path anyone prepares for, and no words can truly explain the depth of such heartache.

Yet whether your loss is that of a child, a spouse, a sibling, or a dearest friend—grief is grief and loss is loss. Each absence leaves a hole nothing in this life can completely fill. And although it may seem hard to believe right now, even in the pitch-black nights of sorrow, tiny rays of hope can still break through. They may come softly, unexpectedly—like a whisper from Heaven reminding you that this is not the end. Just like a book has many chapters, this is not the entire story.

In the pages ahead, it is my heartfelt desire to walk beside you through the winding paths of grief, with Jesus gently leading us through the valley of the shadow of death. Even if you cannot see it now, there is a quiet, life-giving power in grieving well—a strength that transforms sorrow into a deeper trust in Him.

Grieving is not a race to the finish line. It's not something to get over or neatly tie with a bow. It is a lifelong journey, with seasons of deep ache and seasons where peace gently brushes against your heart. Some days you may feel as if you are drowning in sorrow; other days you might be surprised by a laugh or a warm memory that brings a smile. Both are part of healing. I encourage you to give yourself permission to feel every emotion—anger, sadness, confusion, and even joy—without guilt or apology.

You are not alone. Even when your pain feels isolating, others have walked this road. They may not have your exact story, but they understand the language of grief. When the weight becomes too heavy, reach out. Friends, grief support groups, and online communities like Hope During Loss can become lifelines. There is a unique comfort in knowing someone else truly understands.

Over time, you may find that hope does not mean moving on or forgetting your loved one. Hope is learning how to carry your grief and your love together. It's discovering ways to honor their memory—through words, traditions, acts of kindness, or simply living in a way that reflects their impact on your life. Their presence, though unseen, will always be part of you.

Take each day as it comes. Be gentle with yourself. Healing does not erase the pain, but it gives you the strength to breathe, to stand, and to keep going. You are stronger than you think, braver than you believe, and most importantly, you are never walking this path alone.

"The Lord is close to the brokenhearted and saves those who are crushed in spirit."—Psalm 34:18

PRAYER FOR THE JOURNEY

Lord, you see the shattered places in my heart. You
know the pain I carry, the tears I have cried in the dark.
Thank you for being near when my strength is gone.
Help me to hold onto hope—not as a denial of my grief,
but as a reminder that this story is not over. Teach me to
honor my loved one's memory, and to trust that you are
weaving beauty even from the ashes. Amen.

PART ONE

Entering the Waters of Grief

CHAPTER ONE

Navigating the Ocean of Grief

PERHAPS YOU'VE HEARD THAT GRIEF is like the ocean—vast, deep, and ever-changing. One moment, the waters are calm, and you find a sense of peace as memories gently brush the shore of your heart. The next moment, without warning, a storm rolls in, and you're overwhelmed by crashing waves of sorrow and longing. Grief doesn't follow a schedule or respect the passage of time. It simply is—a force of nature that becomes a part of us.

Just like the tides, grief ebbs and flows. Some days are gentle, filled with quiet reflection and a tender ache. Other days feel relentless, like you're being pulled under by currents you can't control. And yet, even in its most turbulent moments, grief speaks to something beautiful: love.

We grieve deeply because we've loved deeply. That love doesn't vanish when someone is gone—it stays with us, woven into the fabric of who we are. Grief is a reminder that love was real, meaningful, and sacred. It tells the story of a bond strong enough to weather storms, even the storm of death itself.

In those early days of loss, it feels like the waves come one after another with little space to breathe. The impact can knock you off your feet, leaving you gasping, wondering how you'll ever find stability again. I remember those first days after Melanie ran ahead to

Heaven. Each wave was fierce, threatening to pull me under. I felt swallowed whole, as if the ocean of grief would never release me.

The grief doesn't disappear, but we learn how to swim within it, to float when we are weary, and to trust that the One who commands the seas is the same One who will see us safely to shore.

But just as in the natural ocean, there are moments when the waters settle. A soft breeze carries calm to the shore, and you can catch your breath. In grief, those moments may be fleeting—a memory that brings a smile instead of tears, or a sunrise that reminds you that beauty still exists. They are glimpses of grace, God's way of reminding us that we are not completely lost at sea.

Grief's waters are not meant to destroy us, though they often feel overwhelming. They are meant to remind us of the depth of love, and the One who anchors us when the waves rage. Scripture tells us in Isaiah 43:2, *"When you pass through the waters, I will be with you; and when you pass through the rivers, they will not sweep over you."* God's presence doesn't promise calm seas, but it does promise that we will not drown. His steady hand holds us even when we feel like we are sinking.

Eventually, we learn how to live with the rhythm of these tides. We recognize that the storms come and go, that waves will rise and fall, and that God's presence is constant regardless of the conditions. The grief doesn't disappear, but we learn how to swim within it, to float when we are weary, and to trust that the One who commands the seas is the same One who will see us safely to shore.

When I walk the beach and watch the endless horizon, I am reminded of eternity—of the promise that this separation is not forever. The ocean stretches farther than I can see, just as God's love stretches beyond death. What feels like endless sorrow today will one day give way to endless joy when we are reunited with those we love. Until then, we learn to live with the waves, to lean on God's strength when our own fails, and to rest in His presence when the waters rise.

Grief, like the ocean, is vast and untamed, but it is not stronger than the One who walks upon the waves.

CLOSING REFLECTION

The ocean of grief may feel vast and unpredictable, but we are never adrift without hope. Each wave that crashes remind us of the depth of our love, and each calm that follows reminds us of God's steady hand. Though the tides shift and storms rise, His presence anchors us, holding us secure when we feel most unsteady. We may not be able to control the waters, but we can trust the One who speaks peace to the storm. And one day, the seas of sorrow will give way to the eternal calm of His presence, where love is perfected and every tear is wiped away.

"He stilled the storm to a whisper; the waves of the sea were hushed." (Psalm 107:29)

PRAYER FOR THE JOURNEY

Lord, in the vast ocean of my grief, be my anchor. When the waters rise and storms rage, steady my heart with Your presence. Teach me to see the beauty in the waves— the proof of the love that still lives within me. Help me to carry that love forward, trusting that You are my lighthouse, guiding me safely through every tide. Amen.

CHAPTER TWO

Grief: A Slow-Motion Nightmare

IF GRIEF IS LIKE THE ocean, vast and unpredictable, there are days when the waves don't just crash against you. Instead, they pull you under, leaving you gasping in a place where nothing feels real. That's when grief begins to feel less like water rising and more like a slow-motion nightmare.

Grief can feel like waking up inside a nightmare that doesn't end when the sun rises. It's as if you are trapped in a dreamscape where everything is distorted and painfully slow. The ordinary routines of life—making coffee, driving to work, laughing with a friend, suddenly feel foreign, heavy, and drenched in sorrow you cannot shake. Even the simplest tasks can feel monumental, as if you are carrying the weight of the world on your back while others around you walk freely.

When grief comes, it disorients us. Life seems blurred, like moving through a fog no one else can see. The world keeps spinning, people carry on with their plans, talking about errands, planning vacations, celebrating milestones, while you struggle just to take the next breath. The nightmare is not only in the loss itself, but in the ache of trying to exist in a world that feels both familiar and completely unrecognizable.

Nightmares often bring a sense of paralysis. You try to run, but your legs won't move. You cry out, but no sound escapes your lips. Grief mirrors that paralysis. You may want desperately to move forward, to feel joy again, to reclaim even a sliver of normalcy, yet you remain stuck, trapped between longing for what once was and facing the painful reality of what is.

Grief may silence our voices, but God hears even the groanings too deep for words.

What makes grief so cruel is its slow-motion nature. Days feel endless, but nights bring little rest. Sleep may come, but it is often interrupted by dreams or memories that stir the ache all over again. Memories replay like haunting visions you cannot turn off, reminding you of what has been lost. A song, a scent, or a photograph can unravel you in an instant, pulling you back into the depths of sorrow without warning.

And yet, even here, tiny glimmers of light begin to break through. Just as the faintest dawn eventually pierces the longest night, moments of grace slip quietly into our pain. A kind word from a friend, a gentle hug, or a verse of Scripture read at just the right time whispers to our weary souls: *you are not alone.*

This is where reliance on God becomes more than a comfort; it becomes a lifeline. When we lean on Him in our brokenness, we begin to discover that we are not powerless in this slow-motion nightmare. Grief may silence our voices, but God hears even the groanings too deep for words. He is not absent in the nightmare. He is present, steady, and unshakable.

When we rely on Him, He steadies our trembling steps and gently leads us forward, even when the way ahead is covered in shadows. Prayer becomes more than a ritual—it becomes the very breath that we breathe. Worship, even through tears, becomes a balm that soothes our weary hearts. His promises become the anchor in the storm, reminding us that this valley of sorrow will not last forever.

His presence transforms the nightmare. Though grief may never fully disappear, it loses its paralyzing grip. The sharpest edges soften, and what once felt like the end of our story unfolds into a new chapter, one marked not only by loss, but also by resilience, faith, and love that endures beyond the grave.

God has a way of redeeming even our darkest seasons. Though we may never "wake up" from the reality of grief, we are not condemned to live forever in its nightmare. By leaning into His strength, we discover that what once felt unbearable can, over time, become bearable—not because the pain vanishes, but because His presence sustains us. Slowly, tenderly, He teaches us how to carry both our sorrow and our love into a future that still holds purpose, meaning, and hope.

The nightmare may not end in the way we wish, but it does not have the final word. God does. And in His hands, even grief becomes a place where His light shines brightest.

Though this journey may feel like a nightmare we cannot wake from, even here God whispers His promise of life and light. And as His presence steadies us in the darkness, we begin to discover that grief, though overwhelming, can also become a holy place where He draws us closer to His heart.

CLOSING REFLECTION

Grief may feel like a nightmare that unfolds in slow motion—distorted, heavy, and seemingly endless. Yet even in the fog, God is present. He sees every tear, hears every unspoken ache, and holds us steady when we feel paralyzed by sorrow. The nightmare does not define the whole of our story. In His hands, even the darkness becomes a canvas for His light, and even the silence becomes a place where His whispers of love can be heard. Though grief lingers, hope rises. And one day, the nightmare will give way to the dawn of His eternal promise—when every tear is wiped away, and His joy makes all things new.

"He will wipe every tear from their eyes. There will be no more death or mourning or crying or pain, for the old order of things has passed away." (Revelation 21:4)

〜〜 PRAYER FOR THE JOURNEY 〜〜

Lord, in the midst of this slow-motion nightmare, I cry out to you. When my steps falter and my spirit feels crushed, remind me of your nearness. Be my anchor when the waves of grief threaten to pull me under. Wrap me in your peace that surpasses all understanding, and guide me out of the shadows into the light of your love. Teach me to lean on you more fully each day, until the nightmare gives way to the dawn of Your eternal promise.

Amen.

CHAPTER THREE

When Grief Feels Unexpected

NOT ALL GRIEF ANNOUNCES ITSELF in advance. Sometimes it arrives suddenly, without warning, shaking the very foundation of our lives. Other times, we may have known loss was coming—through illness, distance, or change—but the moment it actually happens it still takes our breath away. Grief, in many ways, is always unexpected.

It can surprise us with its timing, showing up years after a loss when we thought we had moved forward. So many different things can trigger an avalanche of memories and emotions. When this happens, these moments can feel like ambushes—gentle one moment, gut-wrenching the next.

Sometimes, grief catches us off guard because it appears in situations we don't traditionally label as loss. It might be the grief of a friendship ending, a job change, a dream unfulfilled, or the life we thought we'd have. Each of these can carry a sense of mourning, even if they're not accompanied by a funeral or memorial service. Grief isn't limited to death—it's tied to love, to longing, and to the ache of absence in all its forms.

The unexpected nature of grief can leave us feeling unprepared and vulnerable. We may wonder, *Why am I feeling this way now?* or

Shouldn't I be over this by now? But grief does not follow a calendar. It doesn't consult our schedules, nor does it respect milestones or anniversaries. It has its own rhythm, showing up when something in our heart or surroundings calls it forward.

I can still clearly remember one afternoon, months after Melanie ran ahead to Heaven, standing in the grocery store when it hit me. Nothing about that day suggested it would be different from any other. But suddenly, a simple product on the shelf, a favorite of hers, caught my eye. In an instant, I was taken back to a day long ago. I could see her standing in the aisle, her two long braided pigtails hanging down, looking at the pancake syrup, when she said, "Mrs. Butterworth, I love you." Tears blurred my vision as I gripped the cart, trying to steady myself. I don't know why that memory came rushing back at that precise moment, but the loss I thought I had managed surged back without warning. It was then I realized, grief doesn't wait for an invitation. It enters when love remembers.

Moments like these can be disorienting. We often mistake them for weakness or regression, believing we've gone backward in our healing. But the truth is, these moments are not setbacks. They are reminders. They whisper that love is still alive within us, that memory is still powerful, and that healing does not erase the ache of absence.

Unexpected grief can also be an invitation. It invites us to pause, to remember, to honor what mattered most. A sudden wave of sorrow may hurt, but it can also become a reminder that the bond we shared is not gone. In those moments, instead of pushing grief away, we can learn to embrace it as evidence of love that endures.

Scripture reassures us that God is never caught off guard by the things that catch us by surprise. Long before a memory overtakes us or a tear falls unexpectedly, God already knows. And when grief ambushes us, He is right there—steady, and present in our pain.

Long before a memory overtakes us or a
tear falls unexpectedly, God already knows.

Grief, even when it surprises us, is not meant to destroy us. It can become a place of encounter with God, a chance to lean on Him again, to remember that He is near. When unexpected tears fall, they are noticed, gathered, and cherished by the One who promises to make all things new.

So, if you find yourself caught off guard by sorrow, don't see it as failure. See it as love remembering. Let it be an invitation to pause, to breathe, and to rest in the arms of the God who understands.

CLOSING REFLECTION

Grief often arrives unannounced, surprising us in the ordinary rhythms of life. But each wave, whether sudden or delayed, is a reminder of love's lasting imprint. May we not fear these unexpected moments, but receive them as holy invitations—to remember, to honor, and to lean on the God who is never surprised.

"All the days ordained for me were written in your book before one of them came to be." (Psalm 139:16)

PRAYER FOR THE JOURNEY

Father, when grief catches me off guard, help me not to feel ashamed or discouraged. Remind me that each wave of sorrow is also a wave of love. Teach me to see these moments not as steps backward, but as reminders of the depth of my connection to those I miss. Wrap me in your presence when loss feels fresh again, and let your peace steady my heart. Amen.

CHAPTER FOUR

Letting Time and God Do the Healing

IF YOU'VE EVER BATTLED THE flu or a stubborn cold, you've likely heard the discouraging words from the doctor: *"I'm sorry, but there isn't anything I can do for you. It just needs to run its course."* It's a helpless feeling knowing that the only remedy is time. In many ways, walking through the grief journey is the same. There's no magic formula, no quick-fix, no "three-step plan" to make it disappear. It's a process that takes time, often far more than we expect or want, and there are no shortcuts to work its way through our hearts.

When we lose someone we love, when a relationship ends, or when we endure a life-altering event, our world is upended. The routines, rhythms, and even the sense of security we once knew are suddenly gone. Our new normal doesn't feel normal at all—it feels like a foreign land where nothing looks or feels the same. We may find ourselves desperately searching for relief, only to realize there is no shortcut through the pain. The only way out is through.

But while grief needs to run its course, there are things we can do in the meantime. The first is to give yourself permission to grieve—fully and openly. Let yourself feel the sadness, anger, confusion, or numbness without guilt. Grief doesn't come with a rulebook, and healing is never a straight line. Suppressing or ignoring your emotions doesn't make them go away; it only delays the restoration your heart desperately needs.

Time on its own can dull the sharp edges of grief, but time partnered with God brings true healing.

The second step is to seek connection. While no one else can grieve exactly as you do, being with people who offer genuine care can be a lifeline. Sometimes it's a close friend who will sit with you in silence, other times it may be a support group where you can share openly with people who understand the weight of your sorrow. Even journaling can serve as a form of connection—putting words to the emotions swirling inside can lighten the load you carry. Share your burden, in whatever way works for you.

Most importantly, remember you are never alone. Even when others don't understand, God does. He is not distant in your pain. He draws closer. His presence is constant, His love unshakable, and His comfort deep enough to reach the places words cannot touch. Scripture reminds us in Psalm 56:8 (NLT): *"You keep track of all my sorrows. You have collected all my tears in your bottle. You have recorded each one in your book."* Imagine that—every tear you've shed has been seen, remembered, and held by God Himself.

Time on its own can dull the sharp edges of grief, but time partnered with God brings true healing. He doesn't erase our pain, but He weaves it into our story in a way that eventually brings meaning and even hope. As the days move forward, we begin to notice small shifts. The tears may still come, but they are no longer constant. Memories that once pierced may one day bring a gentle smile. The ache remains, but it softens. This doesn't mean you've moved on—it simply means you are slowly learning to live with your loss in a new way.

I think it's important for us to remember that grief's timeline is unpredictable and deeply personal. Some wounds take longer to heal than others, and no two journeys are alike. What matters most is trusting that God is walking with you through every moment. He is patient with your sorrow, present in your tears, and faithful in your healing. Let time do its work, and let God do His.

CLOSING REFLECTION

Our hearts do not heal overnight, and that is okay. Sorrow needs to run its course, and in the waiting, God is faithful. He is the steady presence that carries us when we are too weak to carry ourselves, the gentle healer who binds our brokenness, and the loving Father who redeems even our deepest pain. As you walk through the valley, trust that both time and God will do their healing work, until one day you look back and see that what once felt impossible has slowly become bearable.

"There is a time for everything, and a season for every activity under the heavens." (Ecclesiastes 3:1)

PRAYER FOR THE JOURNEY

Father, you see the depths of my pain even when I can't express it. I confess I wish this season would pass quickly, yet I choose to trust your perfect timing. Help me to rest in you as grief runs its course, and remind me that every tear I cry is precious to you. Surround me with comfort, send people who will walk alongside me, and keep my heart tender toward your voice. Thank you for being close to the brokenhearted and for carrying me when I feel too weak to stand. In Jesus' name, Amen.

PART TWO

Walking with God
Through the Valley

CHAPTER FIVE

Grief: A Highway of Holiness

NOT LONG AFTER MELANIE RAN ahead to Heaven, I came across a phrase that I scribbled down quickly and tucked into my journal: *Grief: A Highway of Holiness.* I don't remember exactly where I first heard it, but the words stayed with me. They resonated deep in my soul, like a truth waiting to be uncovered. At first, I didn't fully understand them, but as time passed and the Lord walked with me through the valley of sorrow, the weight of those words grew heavier, richer, and more sacred.

There is nothing quite like the sacred nearness of God in the days following deep loss. After Melanie's passing, I didn't just sense His comfort—I experienced His presence in a way I had never known before. It was a holy presence, wrapping around my shattered heart, holding me together when I could not stand on my own.

In the rawness of grief, it's easy to feel like you are wandering aimlessly through a barren wilderness. Nothing makes sense, and even faith can feel fragile. Yet, in the middle of that wilderness, God shows up. His presence is not abstract—it is tangible. It is the comfort that wraps around you at two in the morning when sleep won't come. It is the Scripture verse that leaps off the page and seems written just for you. It is the friend who calls at the exact moment you need to hear another voice.

Grief becomes not just a season of
suffering but also a sacred journey, one
where we are shaped, refined, and drawn
closer to the heart of God

When I think about Jesus, I am comforted by the name Isaiah gave Him: *"a man of sorrows, acquainted with grief."* (Isaiah 53:3) This means that Jesus is not distant from our pain. He knows it intimately. He has walked through betrayal, loss, suffering, and death itself. To walk this highway of holiness with Him is to walk with One who understands. He does not hurry us along the road or minimize our pain; instead, He matches His pace to ours, steadying us when our knees buckle, lifting us when we stumble.

Grief, painful as it is, has a way of opening our hearts to God in ways comfort never could. When we are stripped of illusions, plans, and self-reliance, we find ourselves clinging to Him as our only hope. In those moments, the ground beneath our feet becomes holy, not because we are strong or holy ourselves, but because His holiness meets us there. His presence becomes the pavement on this unchosen road.

This is why I see grief as a highway to holiness—not an escape route, not a detour, but a direct path into the heart of God. In the stillness of sorrow, we see Jesus more clearly. In the ache of longing, we sense His nearness. And in the uncertainty of tomorrow, we lean fully on His righteous right hand.

I'll never forget the early months after Melanie ran ahead to Heaven. There was a holiness in those moments that I could not have explained at the time. The ache was unbearable, but the presence of God was undeniable. I could feel Him near in ways I had never known before. It was not just comfort; it was divine companionship. The tears I cried were sacred to Him, every one collected in His bottle, just as Psalm 56:8 promises.

If you are in the depths right now, know this: it is not your strength that will carry you forward, it is His presence. You are not walking this path alone. Every tear, every sigh, every step is witnessed by the One who understands.

And somehow, through the mystery of grace, He transforms our mourning into something sacred. We may not see it now, but one day we will understand: grief has been not only a valley of shadows, but also a highway to holiness.

Walking this highway of holiness doesn't mean the pain disappears. The sorrow is real and often overwhelming. But what changes is our awareness of the One who walks beside us. Grief becomes not just a season of suffering but also a sacred journey, one where we are shaped, refined, and drawn closer to the heart of God.

And perhaps that is part of grief's mysterious gift. It calls us to a deeper dependence on Him. The things of this world—success, possessions, distractions—begin to fade in importance. What remains is eternal. What remains is the presence of God and the promise of His redemption. The highway of holiness teaches us to fix our eyes not on what is seen, but on what is unseen.

There are still days when the road feels unbearably long, when I want to step off the path and quit altogether. But then I remember: holiness is not about perfection. It is about presence. And the One who promised to never leave or forsake me is the same One who upholds me when my strength is gone.

Grief and loss, painful as it is, can become the very road that leads us closer to God. What feels like the valley of death is transformed into a highway of holiness when Jesus walks with us. And step by step, as He steadies our trembling feet, we discover that even in the midst of deep sorrow, we are standing on sacred ground.

CLOSING REFLECTION

As we journey this holy road with Jesus, we discover that grief is not one feeling but many. In His presence, we are free to bring every emotion—anger, fear, regret, and love—trusting that He can hold them all and begin to heal what feels too heavy for us to carry.

"Cast all your anxiety on Him because He cares for you." (1 Peter 5:7)

⟳⟳⟳ PRAYER FOR THE JOURNEY ⟲⟲⟲

Jesus, Man of Sorrows, thank you for walking this road of grief with me. When the path feels long and my heart is heavy, remind me that you are near. Teach me to see even this valley as holy ground because of your presence. Help me to lean on your strength, to trust in your promises, and to walk with you one step at a time. May this highway of holiness not only draw me closer to you, but also become a testimony of your faithfulness to others who walk this road. Amen.

CHAPTER SIX

Grief: A Symphony of Emotions

WHEN WE THINK OF GRIEF, the first emotion that often comes to mind is sadness. And while sadness is certainly part of the journey, it is far from the whole picture. Grief is not a single note—it is a symphony of emotions, layered and complex, rising and falling in ways that can take us by surprise.

To some it may come as a surprise how closely grief can feel like anger. Sometimes we are angry at the circumstances of our loss, angry at the unfairness of it all, or even angry at God for allowing it to happen. This emotion can erupt when we least expect it, leaving us wondering where it came from and what to do with it.

Other times, grief shows up as anxiety. The future suddenly feels uncertain, fragile, and unsafe. Fear creeps in—fear of more loss, fear of being alone, fear of the unknown. The foundation we once trusted feels shaky, and we find ourselves questioning whether we will ever feel steady again.

Regret is another heavy companion. It whispers what-ifs and should-haves into our minds. We replay conversations and moments, wishing we had said more, done more, loved better. We torment ourselves over things we wish we'd done differently. Alongside regret often comes guilt. Guilt for words left unsaid, or even guilt for moments when we laugh again, as though joy dishonors the depth of our loss.

Then, there is the constant companion of worry, especially when loss shakes the foundation of our security. On top of that, resentment can quietly slip in. Resentment toward those who seem to move on so quickly, or toward a world that carries on as if nothing happened.

Yet, threaded through every one of these emotions is love. That's the heartbeat of grief. We grieve because we have loved, and love does not end when a person's life on earth does. It remains—strong, enduring, unshakable.

Those who haven't walked this journey may not fully grasp how grief touches every corner of life. It changes routines, reshapes relationships, alters how we see the world, and even how we see ourselves. It doesn't arrive in tidy stages or follow a predictable timeline.

This mix of emotions can feel overwhelming. One moment we are crying, the next moment we are irritable, and the next we are quiet and withdrawn. Sometimes, we feel all of it in the same day. The shifting emotional landscape of grief can make us wonder if we are "doing it wrong," but the truth is—this is grief. It doesn't fit neatly into a box, and it isn't meant to.

Understanding that grief is more than sadness allows us to extend grace, to ourselves and to others. Please know this—it's okay to feel a hundred emotions at once. It's okay to not have the words for what you feel. Grief isn't a sign of weakness; it's a reflection of the depth of your love and the fullness of your humanity.

God does not ask us to tidy up our grief or present it to Him in a sanitized way. He invites us to bring it all—the anger, the fear, the guilt, the love. He is not surprised by our emotions, nor is He burdened by them. The psalms remind us that even King David poured out every raw feeling before the Lord, from deep despair to soaring joy. We are invited to do the same. I can't tell you how often I found myself scouring the pages of the psalms. I could so relate to David during this season. One of the things I loved most about him was how he continually ran to the feet of the Father, over and over again.

> God does not ask us to tidy up our grief or present it to Him in a sanitized way. He invites us to bring it all—the anger, the fear, the guilt, the love.
> Eventually, we realize that grief is not an enemy to conquer but a companion to walk with.

When we bring the fullness of our emotions into God's presence, something begins to shift. He may not take them away immediately, but He holds them with us. He reminds us that we are not broken for feeling too much; we are human. And He meets us in that humanity with compassion and grace.

Eventually, we realize that grief is not an enemy to conquer but a companion to walk with. The emotions may continue to ebb and flow, but we begin to trust that they don't have the final say. Beneath them all, God's presence remains steady. He teaches us that it is possible to hold sorrow and joy in the same heart, to cry and to laugh, to ache and to hope, all without guilt.

If you're experiencing the storm of emotions that grief brings, take heart, my friend. You are not alone, and you are not failing. You are walking through a valley that countless others have known, and more importantly, a valley where Jesus Himself walks beside you. He knows the language of tears, the weight of fear, and the cry of love that cannot be silenced. And He promises to carry it with you, one step at a time.

CLOSING REFLECTION

Though the storm of emotions may rage, God's healing touch gently closes the wounds. As time moves forward, the rawness gives way to scars—marks of both suffering and survival, that become testimonies of His faithfulness and love.

"He heals the brokenhearted and binds up their wounds." (Psalm 147:3)

PRAYER FOR THE JOURNEY

Father, you see the full range of my emotions—the anger, the fear, the regret, the love. You know each one before I can even name it. Teach me to bring every feeling to you, without shame or fear. Help me to rest in your understanding, knowing that you created me to love deeply and to grieve honestly. Hold me in the midst of the storm, and remind me that you are my peace. Amen.

CHAPTER SEVEN

The Physical Side of Grief

WHILE GRIEF FLOODS THE HEART with emotions, unfortunately, it doesn't just stop there. Our bodies carry the weight of loss too. Sometimes the heart's ache is mirrored in aching muscles, a racing pulse, or a fatigue that feels bone-deep. Just as grief is more than one emotion, it's also more than an invisible wound—it's a physical experience. To walk this journey well, we must learn to care for both the soul and the body, recognizing that they are deeply intertwined.

When most people think about grief, they focus on the emotional toll—the sadness, anger, and longing that weigh heavy on the heart. But grief doesn't just live in our emotions; it also takes up residence in our bodies. The physical side of grief is real, and it can be just as devastating as the emotional one. I never fully realized how much death and loss affect the body until I found myself sitting in a doctor's office several months after Melanie died. The grief I felt was not only emotional, it had settled into my very bones.

Loss has a way of weaving itself into every fiber of our being. We probably shouldn't be too surprised by this since our minds and bodies are deeply connected, but I have to admit I was shocked by how much the toll of my daughter's death took on me physically. On top of everything else I was feeling, I now felt as if my body was betraying me. When I slept, which was difficult at best, my sleep was restless, and was filled with vivid dreams that left me more exhausted in the morning than when I went to bed. There were times I would still find myself unusually tired, even on the rare occasion of getting a full night's sleep. For many on this journey, some nights may bring insomnia, your body unable to quiet itself because your heart and mind are still wrestling with the pain.

Grief can also bring headaches, muscle tension, chest tightness, or a heaviness that feels almost unbearable. Some people notice changes in appetite—eating far less than normal, or turning to food for comfort. Others experience a racing heart, upset stomach, or waves of dizziness that seem to come out of nowhere. These physical symptoms can be unsettling, especially when you don't connect them immediately to your grief. But they are the body's way of processing the shock of loss. It's your physical self trying to carry the weight your heart is feeling.

Even Scripture acknowledges the physical toll of sorrow. In Psalm 32:3–4, David confessed, *"When I kept silent, my bones wasted away through my groaning all day long. For day and night your hand was heavy on me; my strength was sapped as in the heat of summer."* His words remind us that grief and stress can quite literally sap our strength, leaving us weary in body as well as spirit.

This is why caring for your body during grief is essential. Rest when you need to, even if the world is telling you to keep going. Nourish yourself with food that sustains you, even if your appetite feels off. Get outside, let the sun warm your face, and breathe deeply of the fresh air, reminding you that life continues. Move your body, even in gentle ways—stretching, walking. Small acts of care, repeated over time, can help restore the strength that grief depletes.

Grief doesn't just live in our emotions; it also takes up residence in our bodies.

It is also important to be patient with yourself. Your body is not betraying you—it is simply speaking the language of loss. Fatigue, tension, and aches are all signs that grief is still working its way through. Instead of fighting these signals, listen to them with compassion. Your body is crying out for rest, nourishment, and grace.

The healing of grief is not only an emotional and spiritual journey, it is a physical one too. To honor our grief, we must honor our bodies. They are temples of the Holy Spirit (1 Corinthians 6:19), worthy of care and compassion, even in their weakness. And just as God heals our hearts, He can also restore our physical strength, day by day, as we lean into His presence.

Gradually, you may find that the symptoms ease. The body slowly learns to carry the sorrow with less strain. The sleepless nights grow fewer, and the heaviness begins to lift. Healing may not mean the absence of pain, but it does mean the slow return of strength. Strength that God Himself provides.

CLOSING REFLECTION

Grief affects not only our hearts but our bodies, reminding us of the deep connection between soul and flesh. As we tend to our physical needs with gentleness and patience, we invite God's healing presence into every part of our being. He who formed our bodies knows our pain and promises to restore us—not just in spirit, but in strength.

"He gives strength to the weary and increases the power of the weak." (Isaiah 40:29)

PRAYER FOR THE JOURNEY

Lord, you created my body and know every ache, every tear, and every heavy breath I take. You see the toll grief has taken on my strength and energy. Help me to listen to the needs of my body and not feel guilty for resting. Restore my health in your time and remind me that you are the ultimate healer of both body and soul. Amen.

CHAPTER EIGHT

When the Ordinary Becomes Extraordinary

HINDSIGHT IS ALWAYS 20/20. WHEN our loved ones are no longer with us, there are countless things we find ourselves missing. Surprisingly, it's often not the grand events or milestone celebrations that leave the deepest ache. Instead, it's the small things we once overlooked that become treasures we long for the most.

I think back to my time with Melanie and realize it's not the big vacations or elaborate celebrations that play over and over in my mind. It's the everyday things: the daily and often numerous phone calls—conversations that were sometimes about nothing and everything. It's hearing her laugh echo through the house, watching her sit at the kitchen counter scrolling on her phone, or the way we'd laugh in the nail salon during our mother-daughter mani-pedis. None of those moments would have made a scrapbook page but now, they're priceless treasures. At the time, those moments felt routine, almost forgettable. Today, they shine in my memory like pearls strung together, priceless and irreplaceable.

When grief enters, it sharpens our awareness of just how sacred the ordinary truly is. The routines we once took for granted—the shared meal at the dinner table, the quiet comfort of sitting side by side, all become holy ground when they are gone. These seemingly insignificant moments are the very fabric of life, and when the fabric tears, we realize how much beauty it held.

If you are missing the ordinary moments with your loved one today, know this: your love for them is not diminished by their absence.

It's tempting to dwell on regrets in this space. We ask ourselves questions like, *Did I say "I love you" enough? Did they know how much they mattered? Why didn't I linger longer in those everyday conversations?* Grief can stir up so many questions, leaving us tangled in guilt. But the truth is, none of us live with perfect awareness. We can't possibly know which ordinary moment will be our last with someone we love.

What grief teaches us, however, is how to live differently moving forward. It invites us to slow down and savor the present. It reminds us to pause when our child calls from the other room, to notice the way sunlight spills through the window, to listen fully when a friend shares their heart. Loss sharpens our ability to see the sacred hidden in plain sight.

I've come to believe that ordinary moments are the truest measure of love. They are the building blocks of memory, the daily rhythms that shape our relationships. Grief reminds us of their value and gently nudges us to treasure them with the ones still here. We may not be able to reclaim the moments we've lost, but we can honor them by living more intentionally in the present.

And woven through it all is God's presence. He is in the laughter shared at the dinner table, in the comfort of a hug, in the quiet moments of stillness when our hearts ache. Scripture reminds us that He numbers even the hairs on our head (Luke 12:7). If He pays such attention to what seems small, surely, He is present in the ordinary details of our lives too.

If you are missing the ordinary moments with your loved one today, know this: your love for them is not diminished by their absence. It is alive, woven into your story, carried in the simplest of memories. And one day, when you are reunited, the ordinary will be extraordinary again—each moment radiant with joy in the presence of Christ.

So, hold your memories close. Create more of them with the people still here. Take photos. Linger in conversations. Let the mundane moments matter because one day, they may be the very moments you cherish most.

CLOSING REFLECTION

It is the ordinary moments that shape the story of love. Though grief makes us ache for what is gone, it also teaches us to treasure what remains. May we learn to live with greater awareness, embracing the sacred hidden in the everyday, until the day comes when every ordinary moment is redeemed in eternity.

"Teach us to number our days, that we may gain a heart of wisdom." (Psalm 90:12)

PRAYER FOR THE JOURNEY

Lord, thank you for the gift of ordinary moments—the quiet, unremarkable pieces of life that hold the deepest meaning. Help me to notice them while they're still here and to treasure the people you've placed in my life. Teach me to live with an awareness that every day, no matter how routine, is a gift. May my heart remain grateful for the memories I hold and open to the ones still to come.

Amen

PART THREE

Hope Anchored in Christ

CHAPTER NINE

The Oxygen of Hope

DID YOU KNOW THAT WE can survive without food for about 30 days? A healthy adult can even survive without water for approximately 3–5 days. But living without hope is impossible. Hope is our oxygen. Just as every breath sustains our physical life, hope sustains our spirit. Without it, our souls suffocate under the weight of despair.

When someone we love dies, the air can feel thin, every breath harder to take. Loss has a way of knocking the wind out of us, leaving us gasping for something to hold on to. In those moments, hope becomes not just important, it becomes essential. It is the invisible breath that keeps us from collapsing, the gentle inhalation that whispers, *You can keep going.*

Hope is more than wishful thinking. It is the deep, quiet belief that tomorrow can be better than today, even when today feels unbearable. It is what gives us the strength to press on through challenges, the vision to imagine beauty rising from the ashes, and the courage to take the next step when the road ahead is unclear.

When hope fades, so does our sense of purpose. We can endure almost any trial if we have hope. It lights our way when darkness closes in, helps us rebuild when everything feels broken, and calls us forward when we want to give up.

The challenge is that grief often clouds our vision of hope. When we are deep in sorrow, it can feel out of reach, like a star that shines faintly but seems too far away. Yet Scripture reminds us that hope is not wishful thinking—it is a person. Hope has a name, and His name is Jesus.

> Hope doesn't erase grief, but it changes how we carry it. It reminds us that our story isn't over, that our pain is not wasted, and that one day we will be reunited with the ones we love.

Many place their hope in things that are temporary—success, possessions, or even relationships. While these can bring happiness for a season, they are fragile. When our hope is tied to what can be taken away, it leaves us vulnerable. Jesus offers us a living hope (1 Peter 1:3), one that is not bound by circumstances or swallowed up by death. His resurrection proves that despair never has the final word. Because He lives, we can face tomorrow, even when tomorrow feels unbearably heavy.

In Him, we find more than the promise of a better tomorrow, we find the assurance of forever. His love is constant, His promises are true, and His presence is unending. When the weight of grief is crushing, He becomes our breath. He is the anchor for our souls, holding us steady when the winds rage.

In my own journey, I have found that hope comes in many forms. Sometimes it's as small as a breath prayer whispered through tears: *"Lord, help me make it through today."* Other times it's in the promises of Scripture, words that remind me of God's unchanging faithfulness: *"We have this hope as an anchor for the soul, firm and secure."* (Hebrews 6:19) And sometimes hope comes through community—the embrace of someone who listens without judgment, the quiet presence of a friend who sits with you in silence.

Hope doesn't erase grief, but it changes how we carry it. It reminds us that our story isn't over, that our pain is not wasted, and that one day we will be reunited with the ones we love. For me, hope means knowing I will see Melanie again. It means that the ache of separation is not the end, but only a pause in the greater story God is writing.

Hope also gives us courage to live fully in the present. It allows us to laugh again without guilt, to plan for tomorrow without fear, and to notice the beauty that still surrounds us. It doesn't demand that we deny our pain but invites us to live alongside it with a renewed sense of purpose.

Breathing in hope is an act of faith. Just as our lungs expand to draw in air, so our hearts must be open to receive the truth of God's promises. Some days, hope feels like a deep, satisfying breath. Other days, it is more like gasping for air, but even then, God supplies just enough to keep us moving forward.

Friend, if you're struggling to breathe right now, know this: God has not abandoned you. His Spirit is the very breath that fills your lungs. He will not allow despair to suffocate you. As long as there is breath in your body, there is hope for your soul. His hope fills us again and again, sustaining us until the day when sorrow will be no more.

CLOSING REFLECTION

The streams of God's refreshment carry us through the wilderness, but hope is the oxygen that enables us to truly live again. In grief, hope is not a luxury. It is our lifeline, our anchor, and our promise of joy yet to come.

"We have this hope as an anchor for the soul, firm and secure." (Hebrews 6:19)

PRAYER FOR THE JOURNEY

Lord, thank you for being the very breath of life when grief leaves me gasping. When despair threatens to choke my spirit, remind me that my hope is not in circum- stances but in you. Teach me to inhale your promises, to exhale my fears, and to trust that you are sustaining me moment by moment. Let hope rise within me like oxygen, renewing my strength and pointing me to the day when sorrow will be no more. Fill my spirit with the oxygen of hope, so that even in sorrow, I may live with the assur- ance of your unfailing love. Amen.

CHAPTER TEN

Grieving With Hope

I FIRST HEARD THE TERM *"grieving with hope"* when my pastor called the day after Melanie ran ahead to Heaven. I didn't recall hearing it before, but now I cling to it like a life preserver in stormy seas. Why? Because it means this is not the end. It means I will see my daughter again. It means there will come a day when I wrap my arms around her, look into her beautiful light brown eyes, as I tell her how much I love her and how much I have missed her.

The term comes from 1 Thessalonians 4:13: *"And now, dear brothers and sisters, we want you to know what will happen to the believers who have died so you will not grieve like people who have no hope."* (NLT)

This verse doesn't tell us *not* to grieve. Instead, it tells us how to grieve—with hope. The reality is that while we are on this side of Heaven, there will still be tears, ache, and longing. The death of someone we love leaves an empty place in our hearts, no matter how deeply we trust God's promises. Even as Christians, we are not immune to the deep pain of loss. It's not fear for our loved one's eternity that wounds us, it's their absence from our daily lives.

Grieving with hope means holding two truths in tension. The first truth is the reality of loss—acknowledging the pain, sadness, and longing that come with someone's absence. The second truth is the promise of reunion—the anchor that steadies us in the storm, reminding us that in Christ, death is not the end.

When I think of grieving with hope, I picture a tightrope stretched across the valley of sorrow. On one side is pain, on the other is promise. Hope is the balance pole that steadies us as we cross. Without hope, we tumble into despair. With hope, even when our steps are shaky, we keep moving forward, one step at a time.

Friends, we must normalize grief. There is no shame in mourning. There is no time limit on tears. Grieving too much or too long is a myth. Each journey is unique, and love is not measured by how quickly we move forward. We will always carry our loved ones in our hearts, no matter how much time passes. Hope doesn't erase grief. It infuses it with endurance, reminding us that the story isn't over yet.

I think of Revelation 21:4, which promises, *"He will wipe every tear from their eyes, and there will be no more death or sorrow or crying or pain."* Until that day comes, tears will be part of our story. But those tears are not wasted. They water the soil where hope grows, where faith deepens, and where we learn to walk each day trusting the One who holds the future.

To grieve with hope is to live in the "already and not yet." Already we have the assurance of salvation, already we know Christ has overcome death, already we believe we will see our loved ones again. But we are not yet free from sorrow. We are not yet whole. And so, we grieve—but we grieve as those who know the best is still to come.

Grieving with hope means holding two truths in tension. The first truth is the reality of loss—The second truth is the promise of reunion.

CLOSING REFLECTION

Grief and hope are not enemies—they walk hand in hand. Our sorrow reminds us of love that endures, and our hope reminds us of joy yet to come. To grieve with hope is to live with eyes fixed on eternity, trusting the One who conquered death and promises life everlasting.

"We have this hope as an anchor for the soul, firm and secure." (Hebrews 6:19)

PRAYER FOR THE JOURNEY

Father, thank you for the hope we have in Jesus—the hope that anchors our hearts in the storms of grief. Help me hold fast to the promise of reunion, even on the days when the ache feels unbearable. Teach me to live fully in the present, trusting that your plan is good and that one day, every tear will be wiped away. Until then, help me grieve with hope, clinging to your promises and walking each day with faith. Amen

CHAPTER ELEVEN

Grieving With Grace

AS THE DAYS TURN INTO weeks, and the weeks into months, time begins to take on a strange new rhythm in the wake of loss. Eventually, the years begin to pass too, and yet the ache in your heart can still feel as sharp as it did in the beginning. If you're navigating the journey of grief, whether fresh or years in the making, I want to remind you of something simple but powerful: moving forward requires courage. It takes grit to face the world when your heart feels broken, and strength to live each day while carrying the weight of loss.

Grief demands grit. It takes courage to get out of bed when the weight of sorrow presses heavily on your chest. It takes strength to face milestones and holidays when the empty chair at the table screams louder than the laughter around you. It takes resilience to keep living—really living—when part of you feels like it stopped the day your loved one left.

Grace, however, does not mean pretending the pain is gone or forcing ourselves to be strong in the way the world often expects. True grace is a gift from God—it is His strength poured into our weakness, His mercy covering our flaws, His peace calming our restless hearts. To grieve with grace is to lean on Him when we have no strength of our own.

People may say things like, "You should be moving on by now," or "Aren't you over that yet?" There is no expiration date on love, and therefore, no timeline on grief. As a mother with a daughter in Heaven, I know this all too well. There are still days when the tears come unannounced, and I've learned to welcome them as part of my love story with my daughter.

Perhaps one of the most beautiful aspects of grace in grief is the way it allows us to carry our loved one's memory forward with tenderness rather than anguish.

There have been countless days on my own journey when I have felt utterly emptied, convinced I had nothing left to give. The tears would come without warning, the exhaustion would weigh me down, and the thought of facing another day felt overwhelming. And yet, somehow, I kept moving forward. Looking back, I realize it was not my strength at all—it was God's grace carrying me. His Word tells us, *"My grace is sufficient for you, for my power is made perfect in weakness."* (2 Corinthians 12:9)

Grace allows us to be honest about our pain while still pressing on. It allows us to hold our tears in one hand and our hope in the other. It gives us permission to fall apart when we need to, knowing that God is the One holding us together. And it helps us rise again, day after day, even when grief threatens to undo us.

But grieving with grace also means giving grace—to ourselves and to others. Too often, we judge our own grief harshly, wondering if we are too much for those around us or if we should be further along by now. Grace reminds us that there is no timeline for healing and no right way to grieve. Each step forward, no matter how small, is an act of courage.

It also means extending grace to those who may not understand our grief. Friends and family, often well-meaning, may say things that wound us. They may avoid the subject altogether because they don't know what to say. Grieving with grace allows us to forgive their shortcomings, recognizing that not everyone can comprehend the depth of our loss.

Perhaps one of the most beautiful aspects of grace in grief is the way it allows us to carry our loved one's memory forward with tenderness rather than anguish. Grace softens the sharp edges of sorrow, making space for moments of gratitude, joy, and even laughter again. It doesn't erase the loss, but it transforms the way we live with it, teaching us to carry it with dignity, strength, and love.

To grieve with grace is not to move on, but to move forward—to live fully while still honoring the one we miss. It is walking with courage through the valley of sorrow, trusting that God's grace will be sufficient for every step. And in doing so, our very lives become a testimony of His sustaining power.

If you are in the midst of deep grief, I want you to know that grace is not something you have to muster on your own. It is a gift, freely given by a loving God who sees your broken heart. Let His grace cover you, strengthen you, and guide you as you walk this path. And when the day comes when you look back and realize you have survived what once felt impossible, you will know this—it was His grace all along.

CLOSING REFLECTION

Grieving with grace means living each day with courage, leaning not on our own strength but on the God who carries us. His grace steadies our trembling steps, softens the ache of loss, and gives us strength to live with hope and love. May we walk forward, not perfectly, but faithfully, sustained by His endless grace.

"My grace is sufficient for you, for my power is made perfect in weakness." (2 Corinthians 12:9)

PRAYER FOR THE JOURNEY

Lord, when the weight of grief feels too heavy, remind me of the strength you've placed within me. Give me courage to keep taking steps forward, even when my heart aches. Help me to honor my loved one's memory with grace, to follow the path you've set before me, and to trust that each day you walk beside me. Amen.

CHAPTER TWELVE

Standing Through the Tears

A FEW YEARS AGO, ON a warm, sunny Saturday afternoon I was in the kitchen preparing dinner, chopping vegetables at the kitchen island while music played softly in the background. It was one of those days that seemed made for gathering with friends, and for a little while, life felt lighter again. I was grateful.

A song began to play, one I had never heard before. Without warning and within seconds, the lyrics pierced my heart, and tears began to flood my eyes, streaming down my face. I stood at the counter, knife in hand, as I began to unravel. One moment I was fine, and the next I was completely undone. Grief is unpredictable and it had caught me off guard, reminding me that sorrow often arrives uninvited.

Like a glutton for punishment, I asked Alexa to replay the song—again and again. Then, by the fifth time, something shifted. My tears still flowed, but a quiet peace began to weave through them. The song felt like a window into Heaven, and I could almost picture Melanie—whole, radiant, and free. In that moment, grief and hope coexisted, tangled together in my heart.

That afternoon reminded me of an important truth: sometimes, the bravest thing we can do is stand through the tears. Grief doesn't wait for a convenient time. It interrupts the ordinary, while cooking, driving, shopping, or folding laundry. Anything can activate our grief, stopping us in our tracks, pulling sorrow to the surface once more.

Standing through the tears requires grit. It takes courage to stay upright when sorrow presses heavily on the soul.

To stand through the tears is not to deny grief. Instead, we give it permission to flow, even in the middle of chopping vegetables, and to trust that tears are not weakness but evidence of love. It is allowing sorrow to have its place while continuing to live within the rhythms of daily life. Dinner still needs to be made, friends still gather, the world still turns and somehow, in the middle of it all, we are both grieving and living.

This is the paradox of grief: we carry on while our hearts still ache. Some days we laugh, other days we weep, and sometimes we do both in the same breath. Neither is wrong. Our tears testify that love remains, even when absence stings.

Standing through the tears requires grit. It takes courage to stay upright when sorrow presses heavily on the soul. It takes strength to admit that we are vulnerable and still keep moving forward. But here is what I've learned: the strength to stand doesn't come from us alone—it comes from God.

Psalm 34:18 promises, *"The Lord is close to the brokenhearted and saves those who are crushed in spirit."* That day in my kitchen, I felt His nearness. God didn't rush me past my tears or ask me to hold them back. He simply stood with me; His presence as real as the song echoing through the room.

As time has gone by, I've come to see that standing through the tears is itself a testimony. Each tear that falls is noticed by God. Each moment we choose to keep living, keep breathing, and keep trusting, even with sorrow on our faces, is proof of His sustaining grace. Our grief does not disqualify us from strength; it reveals that His strength is holding us when ours runs out.

So, if you find yourself undone in the middle of an ordinary day, let the tears come. Let them fall while you stand, knowing that God is standing with you. He gathers every tear, He steadies every trembling heart, and He promises that one day, tears will be no more. Until then, His grace is enough to carry us—standing, crying, and living all at once.

CLOSING REFLECTION

Grief has a way of surprising us, often in the middle of ordinary life. But to stand through the tears is to declare that sorrow is not the end of the story. God sees every tear, holds every heart, and strengthens us to keep standing until the day He wipes every tear from our eyes.

"You keep track of all my sorrows. You have collected all my tears in your bottle." (Psalm 56:8)

PRAYER FOR THE JOURNEY

Heavenly Father, thank you for being with me in both my joy and my sorrow. Help me to stand, even when tears fall, knowing that you hold me steady. Remind me that my loved one's pain is gone, and that one day I will see them again. Give me grit to press on, courage to face each day, and faith to believe you are carrying me forward.

Amen.

PART FOUR

Scars, Strength, and Redemption

CHAPTER THIRTEEN

When Scars Become Stories

THERE IS A SACRED BEAUTY in the way God transforms pain. The sharp, unrelenting ache of fresh loss eventually softens into a scar—a lasting reminder of where we've been and what we have endured. While the scar remains, the wound is no longer raw, and over time, those scars begin to speak. They tell of love that cannot be broken, of faith that refused to let go, and of a God who walks with us through the deepest valleys.

I'll never forget the first time I heard the phrase, *"Wounds become scars, and scars become stories."* I was attending my women's group when those words were spoken, and they stopped me in my tracks. They perfectly captured my own experience of grief. Although it certainly took some time and a lot of grief work, the wounds that once consumed me have been knit together by God's healing touch. Now they serve as chapters of my story—chapters I never imagined I would speak of, but ones that can be shared as a testimony of hope.

One of the many things I've learned along this journey is that scars are not a sign of weakness. They are proof that we survived. They remind us that though the wound was deep, it did not destroy us. Each scar whispers that healing has taken place, even if the process was slow and painful. Scars are not meant to erase the memory of the wound, but to transform it into something that points to life beyond the pain.

In the world's eyes, scars may look like blemishes, flaws, or evidence of brokenness. But in God's eyes, scars are redeemed places. They are evidence of His healing power, a visible reminder that what was once unbearable can, through His presence, become bearable. The scars of grief are not pretty, but they are holy. They mark us as people who have walked through the fire and found God faithful in the flames.

Even Jesus carried scars. After His resurrection, when He appeared to Thomas, He did not hide His wounds. Instead, He invited Thomas to touch them. His scars told the greatest story ever written—that death had been defeated, that hope was alive, and that love had triumphed. If even the risen Savior bore scars, then our scars can also become holy testaments of God's redemptive power.

There are times when I look at the scars of my grief and feel the ache of loss all over again. They are tender reminders of a story I would never have chosen. But there are also times when I look at them and see beauty—a reminder that God has carried me, sustained me, and is weaving my story into something bigger than I can see. My scars have allowed me to connect with others in ways I never could have otherwise. They give me language to comfort those whose wounds are still raw, to say, *"You are not alone. I have walked this road too, and God is with us."*

When scars become stories, they become gifts. They allow us to give away the comfort we ourselves have received. They allow us to bear witness to God's faithfulness, to shine light into someone else's darkness, and to remind the world that healing is possible.

The scars of grief are not pretty, but they are holy. They mark us as people who have walked through the fire and found God faithful in the flames.

Your scars, like mine, may still feel tender. But one day you will look at them and realize that they are not only marks of what you have lost, but also of what you have gained—faith, resilience, compassion, and the unmistakable presence of God. They are not the end of your story; they are the very places where His story of redemption shines the brightest.

Healing is possible. Restoration is real. And the truth remains; wounds can heal, scars can testify, and stories can point to the goodness of God.

CLOSING REFLECTION

Scars remind us of where we've been, but God also promises refreshment for where we are going. In the barren wilderness of grief, He brings streams in the desert—unexpected moments of renewal that sustain us on the journey.

"I will make a way in the wilderness and rivers in the desert." (Isaiah 43:19)

PRAYER FOR THE JOURNEY

Father, thank you for the healing you bring, even when it comes slowly and through many tears. Help me to see my scars not as marks of defeat, but as reminders of your faithfulness and love. Teach me to share my story with courage, so that others may find hope in you. May my scars point always to your glory and to the redemption that is possible through Christ. Amen.

CHAPTER FOURTEEN

When Scars Speak Hope

SCARS ARE NEVER WASTED IN God's hands. They not only remind us of His grace in our own lives, but they also carry a voice that can reach beyond us. What begins as a personal testimony of survival and faithfulness can become a story that whispers courage to others walking through their own valleys. Our scars, though born of pain, have the power to speak hope. And that is where the journey continues.

Scars tell stories. They are visible reminders that something once hurt us, but it did not destroy us. They are proof of both suffering and survival. A scar says: *I endured, I healed, I am still here.* In the same way, the unseen scars of grief, the tender places in our hearts left behind by loss, carry their own kind of testimony. While they may never fully fade, they can speak hope, both to us and to others.

When Thomas doubted, Jesus didn't hide His wounds. Instead, He invited Thomas to see and touch them: *"Put your finger here; see my hands. Reach out your hand and put it into my side. Stop doubting and believe"* (John 20:27). His scars were not marks of defeat, but of victory—evidence of His love, His sacrifice, and His triumph over death. His scars still speak today, telling the story of a Savior who conquered death and offers life everlasting.

Our scars, far from being blemishes, can become sacred places where hope speaks most clearly.

In much the same way, the scars left by grief can become places where God's power and grace are revealed. They remind us of love so deep that it cannot be forgotten. They remind us of the valleys we thought we could not survive, but did. And they remind us that healing is possible, even if it leaves marks. Our scars, far from being blemishes, can become sacred places where hope speaks most clearly.

When others see our scars, they see not only what we endured, but also the faithfulness of the God who carried us. A mother who has lost a child but continues to walk forward with courage speaks volumes to others in pain. A father who grieves deeply yet still clings to hope testifies to God's sustaining strength. A person who has endured great loss but continues to live with compassion and kindness becomes a living picture of grace. These are the stories our scars tell—stories of hope, whispering to others: *You can survive this too. You are not alone.*

Sharing our scars requires vulnerability. It means being willing to let others see where we've been broken. It asks us to resist the temptation to cover up or pretend we've never struggled. But it is often in that very sharing that others find the courage to keep walking. Our scars may be personal, but their testimony is powerful. When scars speak hope, they become bridges of connection, reminders that grief is universal, but so is the presence of God's grace.

Sometimes, our scars even speak hope back to our own hearts. When fresh waves of grief return, looking back on how God has already carried us through difficult seasons becomes a source of strength. Each scar declares: *You've been here before. You survived then. God was faithful then, and He will be faithful now.* In this way, scars are not just passive reminders but active voices—speaking encouragement when despair tries to silence us.

I have come to see that our scars will never make us who we were before loss. They are not meant to erase the past or return us to a version of ourselves untouched by sorrow. But they can shape us into people marked by resilience, empathy, and grace. Our scars soften us toward others who are hurting, reminding us that pain is universal, but so is the possibility of healing. And in the hands of Jesus, they become more than reminders of pain—they become testimonies that speak hope and redemption.

The scars of grief show that while life may have broken us, God's love has held us together. Like Jesus, we do not need to hide them. We can hold them out with honesty, letting them bear witness to both the suffering and the Savior who redeems. And just as His scars declared eternal victory, ours can declare that even in loss, hope still lives.

CLOSING REFLECTION

When scars speak hope, they remind us that pain does not have the final word. Each mark becomes a testimony—of survival, of love that still endures, and of a God who never abandoned us in the valley. May we listen to what our scars are saying, and may we have the courage to let them speak hope into the lives of others who wonder if they can endure too.

"But I will restore you to health and heal your wounds, declares the Lord." (Jeremiah 30:17)

PRAYER FOR THE JOURNEY

Lord, thank you for transforming my scars into stories of hope. Teach me not to hide the marks of my grief, but to let them reflect your faithfulness and healing. Give me courage to share my story so others may find comfort and strength. May my scars always point to you, the One who carried me through and who continues to make all things new. Amen.

CHAPTER FIFTEEN

Kintsugi: Beauty in the Broken

WHEN OUR SCARS BEGIN TO speak hope, something remarkable happens: they no longer look like flaws, but like lines of beauty. In Japan, there is an ancient art form called *kintsugi*, which means "golden joinery" that mirrors this truth in a breathtaking way. When a ceramic bowl or vase is broken, rather than discarding it, the pieces are gathered and carefully mended with lacquer mixed with powdered gold. The cracks are not erased, they are illuminated, transformed into gleaming veins of beauty. The once-broken vessel is not only restored but is considered even more valuable because of its scars. And so, it is with us, when Christ fills our brokenness with His grace.

Grief makes us feel like those shattered vessels. Loss has a way of breaking us into pieces. Our hearts are fractured, our lives changed, and our sense of self scattered. In the first tender days of grief, it may feel impossible to imagine ever being whole again. We may even believe that our brokenness has ruined us beyond repair. But this is where the gospel whispers hope. Jesus, the One who binds up the brokenhearted, is the Master Artist who gathers our pieces and begins the slow work of putting us back together again.

Like *kintsugi*, He doesn't erase our cracks. Instead, He redeems them. The places where we are most broken become the very places where His grace shines brightest. Our scars, far from making us less valuable, reveal the story of His healing touch. As Paul wrote in 2 Corinthians 12:9, *"My grace is sufficient for you, for my power is made perfect in weakness."* What feels like weakness to us becomes a canvas for His strength.

In my own grief, I often longed to return to who I was before loss shattered me. I wanted to be "whole" in the way I used to understand it. But over time, I began to realize that healing does not mean going back to what was. It means becoming remade into someone new—someone shaped by both sorrow and grace. Like a vessel repaired with gold, I am not the same as before. Yet, perhaps, because Christ's presence fills the cracks of my brokenness with His light, I am even more radiant than I once was.

Kintsugi teaches us to see brokenness not as an ending, but as an opportunity for transformation. In the same way, grief does not mean our lives are over, though it may feel that way in the darkest moments. With the Shepherd's care, our hearts are slowly reassembled, scarred but sacred, marked but meaningful.

The scars of grief become sacred stories. They tell of a love deep enough to wound and a God faithful enough to restore. They remind us that the cracks of our lives are not shameful, but holy places where grace has done its most powerful work. As Isaiah 41:10 promises, *"So do not fear, for I am with you; do not be dismayed, for I am your God. I will strengthen you and help you; I will uphold you with my righteous right hand."* His strength is poured into us not in spite of our brokenness, but because of it.

We may never look or feel quite the same again. Grief changes us. But change does not mean ruin. In Christ, change can mean renewal.

We may never look or feel quite the same again. Grief changes us. But change does not mean ruin. In Christ, change can mean renewal. Our cracks, our scars, our fragile places become filled with

His golden grace. We are still here. We are still held. And we are still beautiful in His eyes.

Like *kintsugi,* our healing takes time. The artist's work is patient and precise, restoring us piece by piece. And though the process may hurt, the finished vessel, the life marked by both sorrow and grace, is a testimony that beauty truly can emerge from brokenness. And while we will always carry the lines of loss within us, those lines tell the story of love, survival, and a faithful God.

CLOSING REFLECTION

We are all vessels, fragile and prone to breaking. Yet in God's hands, our cracks do not diminish us—they reveal the brilliance of His redeeming love. May we learn to see our scars not as flaws, but as golden lines of grace, testifying to the One who brings beauty from brokenness.

"But we have this treasure in jars of clay to show that this all-surpassing power is from God and not from us." (2 Corinthians 4:7)

PRAYER FOR THE JOURNEY

Lord Jesus, you see every broken piece of my heart.
Thank you for being the master artist who gathers what
grief has shattered and gently restores me with your
grace. Teach me not to despise my scars, but to see them
as places where your love shines through. Fill the cracks
of my soul with your presence, and let my life reflect the
beauty of your redeeming work. Amen.

CHAPTER SIXTEEN

Grace in the Scars

SCARS TELL THE TRUTH. SOMETHING hurt us deeply, and we were changed by it. They remind us of pain, yet they also testify to survival. But for those who walk with Christ, scars can hold an even greater meaning—they can become places where grace is most visible.

After His resurrection, Jesus bore the marks of the cross on His hands and side. He did not erase them when He stepped out of the tomb. Instead, He carried His scars into eternity, transforming them from symbols of suffering into signs of victory. His scars told the story of sacrifice, love, and redemption. They became proof that death was not the end, and that grace had triumphed.

In our grief, we carry scars of our own. They may not be visible to others, but they mark our hearts and our lives. At first, they may feel like disfigurements—painful reminders of loss that set us apart from those who cannot understand the depth of our sorrow. But as we move forward with the tender work of Christ, these scars can begin to reveal something more—the unmistakable imprint of God's grace.

Grace in the scars does not mean we no longer feel sorrow. It does not erase longing or silence every tear. Instead, it means that even within our pain, God's presence has been faithful. It means that what once threatened to destroy us has become a place where

His love holds us together. Just as *kintsugi* fills broken pottery with veins of gold, grace fills the cracks of our broken hearts with the presence of Christ. We are still marked, but we are also made new.

Grace in the scars means that rather than closing us off, our wounds open us up to love others more deeply. We become living reminders that healing is possible—not because the pain disappeared, but because God entered into it with us.

I have learned that my scars carry stories of both love and survival. They remind me of the depth of my loss, but they also remind me of the depth of God's comfort. They testify that even when I felt most shattered, He did not abandon me. When I doubted I could endure another day, His grace was the strength that sustained me. And when I feared that grief would consume me, His peace gently steadied me. My scars may remain, but they shine with the truth that God was, and still is, very present in my pain.

Our scars also become instruments of empathy. They allow us to walk beside others with compassion because we know the path they are traveling. Grace in the scars means that rather than closing us off, our wounds open us up to love others more deeply. We become living reminders that healing is possible—not because the pain disappeared, but because God entered into it with us.

And isn't that what grace does? It steps into the broken spaces of our lives, not to deny them but to redeem them. Grace takes the parts of us we would rather hide and transforms them into testimonies of His love. In this way, our scars become sacred—they are not just personal reminders, but proclamations of God's sustaining presence.

Sometimes, I still look at my scars—those tender places in my soul that loss has carved—and feel the ache of what will never be again. But then I remember: Jesus still carries His scars too. They were not erased in His resurrection; they became eternal evidence of His love. If the Savior of the world chose to keep His scars, perhaps mine are not marks of shame at all. Perhaps they are marks of grace, shining with the story of His faithfulness.

In the end, scars are not signs of weakness, but of grace. They tell the story of a God who redeems, who heals, and who makes beauty out of brokenness. And though they remain, they do not diminish us. Instead, they remind us of the One who was scarred for us, and whose love is forever etched into our lives.

CLOSING REFLECTION

Grace in the scars reminds us that even what once broke us can become a place where God's presence is revealed. Our scars whisper of survival, speak of love, and shine with redemption. May we learn to see them not as flaws, but as evidence of grace—the grace of Christ, who still carries His own scars as proof of love everlasting.

"For it is by grace you have been saved, through faith—and this is not from yourselves, it is the gift of God." (Ephesians 2:8)

PRAYER FOR THE JOURNEY

Lord, thank you for the grace that fills the scars of my life. Help me to see them not as marks of shame or weakness, but as reminders of your healing presence. Let my scars testify to your love, both in my heart and to others who are hurting. May every mark of my grief become a place where your grace shines through. Amen.

CHAPTER SEVENTEEN

Redeemed by Love

REDEMPTION IS ONE OF THE most powerful truths of the gospel. To redeem means to buy back, to restore, to bring value where it once seemed lost. It is the heartbeat of God's story—taking what is broken, wounded, or ruined and making it new. For those of us who grieve, redemption feels like an impossible promise. How can something so painful, so devastating, ever be made new? And yet, through Christ, even our grief can be redeemed—not erased, but transformed by His love.

When Jesus laid down His life on the cross, He entered into the deepest human suffering. His love was not abstract; it was poured out in blood and tears. The resurrection was not just victory over death—it was the ultimate redemption. What seemed like the end became the beginning. What looked like defeat became triumph. Through His sacrifice, Jesus proved that love is stronger than death. His redeeming work is not only about eternal salvation, but also about breathing new life into our present brokenness.

In our own lives, grief often feels like an unredeemable loss. The one we love is gone, the life we knew has been shattered, and nothing can return it to what it once was. The silence left in the wake of death can feel final. But here is where the power of God's redeeming love shines brightest: He does not discard us in our sorrow. Instead,

He enters into it with us, holding our broken hearts and whispering that this is not the end of the story. Redemption is His specialty.

Redemption in grief does not mean forgetting. It does not mean pretending the loss never happened. It means God takes even our deepest ache and begins to bring forth something meaningful. It may look like newfound compassion for others who are hurting. It may be the strength to encourage someone who feels hopeless. It may be a deeper intimacy with God, born out of the nights we cried to Him in desperation. Redemption transforms the wound into a well of grace—where what once brought only sorrow begins to over-flow with love.

In my own journey, I have seen glimpses of redemption in ways I never expected. Out of heartbreak came opportunities to walk alongside others in their grief. Out of emptiness came a new aware-ness of God's presence that I might have missed otherwise. Out of brokenness came a faith not untouched by sorrow, but strength-ened because of it. None of this totally removes the ache of missing Melanie, but it reminds me that love has the last word, and that God's love is powerful enough to redeem even what I thought was beyond repair.

Redeemed by love means that our stories don't end with loss. They continue with God's favor. Our lives become testaments not only to what we have endured, but to the God who is able to weave beauty out of ashes. His redeeming love restores our hope, renews our strength, and reminds us that death does not have the final say.

Redemption in grief does not mean forgetting. It does not mean pretending the loss never happened. It means God takes even our deepest ache and begins to bring forth something meaningful.

The prophet Isaiah spoke words that ring true for every griev-ing heart: *"The Redeemer will come to Zion, to those in Jacob who repent of their sins, declares the Lord."* (Isaiah 59:20) Redemption is not a distant hope but a present reality. God's redeeming love meets us here and now—in the very places we feel most undone.

Love redeems us because love Himself walked into death, bore its sting, and emerged victorious. This same love is at work in us today. Although it doesn't erase our grief, it does infuse it with purpose, allowing beauty to emerge where there was once only brokenness.

CLOSING REFLECTION

Redeemed by love, our scars no longer speak only of pain, they also tell the story of grace. God does not waste our sorrow; He transforms it into testimony. May we trust Him with the broken places, believing that His redeeming love is strong enough to weave beauty out of ashes and life out of loss.

"He has delivered us from the dominion of darkness and brought us into the kingdom of the Son He loves, in whom we have redemption, the forgiveness of sins." (Colossians 1:13–14)

PRAYER FOR THE JOURNEY

Lord, thank you for your redeeming love that meets me in my grief. Teach me to trust that even my deepest pain is not beyond your reach. Redeem the broken pieces of my story and transform them into something that brings life, hope, and compassion. Let my life reflect the power of your love, and may others see through me that you are the God who makes all things new. Amen.

CHAPTER EIGHTEEN

From Sorrow to Strength

EVEN THOUGH MELANIE HAS BEEN gone for several years now, there are still moments when it often feels both like yesterday and forever since I've seen her. Time, they say, is a funny thing—but when it comes to the moment your child leaves this earth, there is nothing funny about it. A parent is never meant to outlive their child, and the ache that comes with it is something words can never fully capture.

When the ache was still so fresh, I became laser-focused on the question that haunted me: W*hy*? I asked it over and over again, desperate for an answer that would make sense of the unbearable. But the answer never came. What I discovered instead was that God was not asking me to understand, but to trust Him. Then, as time passed by, through prayer, surrender, and His gentle whisper, I stopped demanding the *why*. I began to believe there was a greater plan, one I may never fully grasp on this side of Heaven.

God has been faithful to show me that even in the hardest places, He is leading me from sorrow to strength. He has not erased the grief, but He has taught me that it can coexist with hope. Isaiah 61:3 reminds us of His promise *"to bestow on them a crown of beauty instead of ashes, the oil of joy instead of mourning, and a garment of praise instead of a spirit of despair."* This is not just poetic language—it is the miracle of what God does when we place our sorrow in His hands.

Choosing joy in grief changes the landscape of this journey. It means deciding to remember the love more than the loss and to see the fingerprints of God's grace in the middle of the pain.

Along this path, He has placed people in my life whose own stories of loss and healing have given me hope. Through shared tears, testimonies, and prayers, we have become lifelines for one another. Their scars remind me that I am not alone, and my own story allows me to speak life into someone else's pain. In these exchanges, I see God's redemptive hand, taking what the enemy meant for harm and turning it into a testimony of His faithfulness.

Choosing joy in grief changes the landscape of this journey. It means deciding to remember the love more than the loss and to see the fingerprints of God's grace in the middle of the pain. When I think of Melanie's smile, her laughter, and the way she made people feel seen, those memories become gifts I can unwrap again and again. They are reminders that love endures, even across the veil of death.

My faith has been the anchor holding me steady in these years of grief. For me, the only way to stand was to first fall to my knees. Prayer has been my posture of surrender. I'm reminded of the words from a song by Phil Wickham: *"When I fight, I'll fight on my knees, with my hands lifted high. Oh God, the battle belongs to You."* It is there, in surrender, that God's light breaks through the shadows.

I've carried Melanie forward in tangible ways as well. Around my neck hangs a necklace imprinted with her thumbprint, engraved with the words: *"I will carry you with me in my heart always."* It rests over my heart as both a comfort and a reminder that her life continues to ripple outward in mine.

I have often said, only God could take one of the worst things that could happen and turn it into something that reflects His glory. With every word I write, with every story I share, Melanie's life continues to touch people across places I've never even been. My grief has become both a wound and a witness. And this, I believe, is just a small part of the story God is still writing—from sorrow to strength.

CLOSING REFLECTION

Grief may begin in sorrow, but in God's hands it does not end there. His presence transforms our weakness into strength, our mourning into endurance, and our brokenness into a testimony of His faithfulness. May we hold tightly to this truth: sorrow is real, but so is the strength that comes from Christ.

"The Lord gives strength to His people; the Lord blesses His people with peace." (Psalm 29:11)

PRAYER FOR THE JOURNEY

Heavenly Father, thank you for being close to the brokenhearted. Thank you for making beauty from the ashes of my life. Help me to remember the love more than the loss, to choose joy over despair, and to trust in the hope that is only found in you. Teach me to carry my daughter's memory as a light in this world, reflecting your grace. Until the day we are reunited, keep my heart steadfast and my eyes fixed on Jesus. Amen.

PART FIVE

God's Comfort and Presence

CHAPTER NINETEEN

The Oil of Joy

GRIEF HAS A WAY OF stripping life of its color. The world can feel gray, muted, and unbearably heavy. Moments that once brought delight seem hollow. Laughter feels far away, almost foreign, as if it belongs to a life we can no longer touch. Yet in Isaiah 61:3 we encounter one of the most tender promises of God: *"to bestow on them...the oil of joy instead of mourning."* This is not a denial of sorrow, but a declaration that joy, even in the deepest valleys, is possible through Him.

In the ancient world, oil was a symbol of blessing, refreshment, and healing. It was poured over weary travelers to restore them after long journeys. It was used in anointing ceremonies to set people apart for God's purpose. It was woven into daily life as a source of strength and vitality. When Isaiah speaks of "the oil of joy," he reminds us that joy is not something we conjure up or manufacture. It is not dependent on circumstances, nor is it the absence of grief. It is a divine gift—something God pours over us like oil, a healing balm for broken hearts.

For those who grieve, joy can feel impossible. Mourning settles like a heavy garment, and it is difficult to imagine ever living without its weight. The thought of laughing, smiling, or feeling gladness again can even stir guilt. But God does not ask us to create joy on our own. He anoints us with it. Like oil, it seeps into the cracks of our pain, softening what feels hardened, restoring what feels withered, and bringing light to what feels unbearably dark.

The oil of joy does not erase mourning, it transforms it. It allows us to carry grief and joy together, hand in hand.

I can remember the first time I truly laughed after my loss. It startled me. For a moment, I felt guilty, as if joy dishonored my grief. If my daughter could no longer laugh, why should I? How could I? But then I began to realize that laughter, smiles, and even simple moments of gladness were not betrayals, they were gifts. They were glimpses of our Father's healing work. They were the oil of joy, poured gently and unexpectedly over my wounded heart.

Joy in grief looks different than joy before loss. It may not be loud or exuberant. It may be quiet, fragile, and momentary at first. Sometimes it comes in a fleeting memory that makes you smile before the tears return. Sometimes it comes in a friend's kindness or in a sunrise that reminds you of God's presence. But even in its gentleness, it carries power. It reminds us that darkness does not own us. It whispers that our loved one's memory can bring smiles as well as tears. And it assures us that God's Spirit is still at work, weaving hope into sorrow.

The oil of joy does not erase mourning, it transforms it. It allows us to carry grief and joy together, hand in hand. It teaches us that we can honor the depth of our loss while also embracing the beauty of life that still remains. It is a holy paradox: mourning may linger, but joy can still break through. Like streams in the desert, it flows into places that once felt barren and lifeless.

In time, this oil of joy becomes part of our testimony. It shows the world that while sorrow is real, it does not have the final word. Love endures. Hope rises. And God's joy, unlike fleeting happiness, sustains us with strength we cannot find on our own. It is the quiet, steady reminder that we are still alive, still held, and still able to experience moments of beauty because of His faithfulness.

CLOSING REFLECTION

The oil of joy does not replace grief, it redeems it. It is God's way of reminding us that even in mourning, His Spirit brings refreshment, healing, and hope. May we learn to receive joy as His gift—never as a betrayal of sorrow, but as a testimony that His presence is greater than our pain.

"You anoint my head with oil; my cup overflows." (Psalm 23:5)

PRAYER FOR THE JOURNEY

Lord, thank you for the oil of joy you pour over my mourning heart. When sorrow feels heavy, remind me that joy is still possible in you. Teach me to receive it without guilt, to embrace it as your gift of healing and grace. May the oil of joy soften my grief, restore my spirit, and shine through my life as a testimony of your faithfulness. Amen.

CHAPTER TWENTY

A Garment of Praise

THE PROPHET ISAIAH PAINTS A picture of God's comfort that is both tender and powerful. As we just talked about one of the promises of God—providing the oil of joy instead of mourning, He doesn't stop there. While joy poured over us is His healing balm—He also gives us a garment of praise instead of a spirit of despair. If the oil of joy restores our hearts from the inside, the garment of praise surrounds us on the outside, covering our despair with hope. Together, they remind us that even in grief, God provides everything we need to endure.

As grievers, we are well aware that grief often feels like despair wrapped around us, heavy and suffocating, as though it clings to every part of life. Despair is not just an emotion—it feels like something we wear, something that weighs on our shoulders and makes every step feel like a burden. But God offers something different. He clothes us with a garment of praise, a covering that shifts our focus from what is lost to the One who never leaves us. Praise does not deny the pain of grief; it surrounds it with the truth of God's presence.

Worship has a way of healing that words alone cannot explain. Music especially has the power to reach places in our souls that nothing else can touch. In seasons of grief, when prayers feel impossible and Scripture feels hard to grasp, a song of worship can slip past the walls of sorrow and minister to the deepest parts of our hearts. It becomes not just a sound, but a covering, a garment woven from truth and hope.

I remember days when the weight of loss felt unbearable, when the silence in my house only magnified the ache in my heart. On those days, my prayers faltered, my words failed, and despair seemed to wrap itself more tightly around me. But when I turned on worship music, something shifted. The lyrics spoke truths I couldn't put into words myself. The melodies carried prayers I could not pray. Sometimes I simply sat and listened, letting the music wash over me like a gentle balm. Other times, I sang through tears, the sound broken but still an offering. In those moments, I experienced what Isaiah meant by a garment of praise. Praise became something I could put on, something that covered my despair with hope and reminded me that God was still worthy of worship, even in my grief.

Worship may not erase pain, but it certainly reframes it. It shifts our gaze from the valley to the Shepherd who walks beside us. It reminds us that we are not defined by our sorrow, but by His faithfulness. Praise is a weapon against hopelessness. Where mourning tries to weigh us down, praise lifts our hearts, even if only for a breath. Where sorrow whispers that joy is gone, praise declares that the Lord still reigns, still loves, and still holds us.

Praise is a weapon against hopelessness. Where mourning tries to weigh us down, praise lifts our hearts, even if only for a breath.

There is a mystery to praise that cannot be explained by logic alone. Something happens when we choose to worship in the valley—it loosens despair's grip. Even when our voices shake and our hearts ache, praise declares truth that despair cannot silence. Worship is not about denying our sadness; it is about declaring that

God is greater than our sadness. And in that declaration, despair loses its power.

Worship is also a pathway to healing because it brings us back to the promises of God's word. Many songs are drawn directly from Scripture, wrapping eternal truths in melody and rhythm. When we sing, or even when we simply listen, we are clothing ourselves in those promises. We are covering our weary souls with a garment that cannot be torn by grief. Over time, that garment becomes familiar. It becomes something we reach for again and again, not because life has grown easy, but because we have learned that death marks a comma, not a period.

God doesn't ask us to praise Him only when life is good. He invites us to praise Him in the valley, because He knows it is there that praise becomes most powerful. It does not change the fact of our grief, but it changes the atmosphere of our hearts. It becomes a covering of peace, a garment that protects us from despair's weight, and a pathway through which His healing love can enter.

Worship is not just something we do—it is something we put on. It is the garment God gives to wrap around His children when despair presses close. And as we wear it, day after day, it slowly begins to transform us, not by removing our grief, but by clothing us in His presence, His truth, and His love.

CLOSING REFLECTION

The garment of praise is God's gift for weary hearts. It does not deny our grief, but it covers us with the reminder that His presence is greater than despair. May we choose to clothe ourselves in worship—even through tears—trusting that praise has the power to lift our gaze, renew our strength, and wrap us in the peace of God's unfailing love.

"Why, my soul, are you downcast? Why so disturbed within me? Put your hope in God, for I will yet praise Him, my Savior and my God." (Psalm 42:11)

PRAYER FOR THE JOURNEY

Lord, thank you for clothing me with a garment of praise when despair feels heavy. Teach me to lean into worship, to let music and song speak when words fail. Cover my spirit with melodies of truth and hope, and let praise become a healing pathway for my heart. May every song I lift, whether whispered through tears or sung with joy. bring glory to you and remind me that I am never alone.

Amen.

CHAPTER TWENTY-ONE

Comforted to Comfort

WHILE WORSHIP LIFTS OUR GAZE and wraps us in God's presence, reminding us that despair does not have the final word, God's design for comfort is never just for us alone. The same God who clothes us with a garment of praise also invites us to extend His comfort outward. What we receive in our sorrow, He intends to flow through us to others who are hurting. And so, the journey continues. not only comforted, but called to comfort.

One of the most precious truths in Scripture comes from Paul's words in 2 Corinthians 1:3–4: *"Praise be to the God and Father of our Lord Jesus Christ, the Father of compassion and the God of all comfort, who comforts us in all our troubles, so that we can comfort those in any trouble with the comfort we ourselves receive from God."*

This verse reveals a beautiful rhythm. God not only comforts us in our grief for our own sake, He also equips us, through that very comfort, to come alongside others. Our pain becomes the soil where empathy grows, and our scars become the bridges that connect us to hurting hearts.

In the early days of grief, it can be hard to imagine ever being able to extend comfort to others. Our sorrow feels all-consuming, and simply surviving the day takes all the strength we have. Yet even then, God's comfort begins to seep into the cracks of our bro kenness. He meets us in our tears, gathers us in His arms, and whispers hope into our despair. And in time, the very comfort that carried us begins to overflow into others.

Our pain becomes the soil where empathy grows, and our scars become the bridges that connect us to hurting hearts.

I have seen this in my own journey. There were people who sat with me in my pain, who didn't try to fix it but simply brought the presence of Christ through their listening, their prayers, and their love. They became living reminders that I was not alone. Later, when someone else walked through the valley of grief, I found myself able to do the same, not because I had all the answers, but because I knew the ache of loss. My own comfort from God became a gift I could pass along, reminding others that they too were not alone.

This is the mystery of God's abiding love: He wastes nothing, not even our sorrow. The comfort we receive is never meant to stop with us. It flows outward, rippling into the lives of others. Sometimes it is through words of encouragement. Other times it is through silent presence, or through sharing a story that says, *"I see you. I understand."* In every case, it is Christ's comfort, not ours, that touches the heart. We are simply the vessels.

Being comforted to comfort does not mean we must be fully healed before we can help. In fact, our ongoing grief often makes our comfort more authentic. It allows us to walk alongside others not as people who have moved on, but as fellow travelers still learning to lean on the Shepherd. Our scars speak of survival, and in that honesty, others find courage. In this way, our sorrow becomes sacred—it deepens our compassion and expands our capacity to love.

I think of how Jesus Himself modeled this truth. In His ministry, He met people in their suffering. He wept at Lazarus's tomb. He touched lepers who had been shunned. He sat with the broken, the weary, and the grieving. His comfort was not distant or shallow—it was born of entering into human suffering with divine compassion. And now, as His followers, He calls us to comfort others with the same heart He has shown us.

As you walk through the hard moments of grief, know this: the comfort God gives you now is not only for today, but also for tomorrow. One day, when the time is right, He may use your story, your tears, and your scars to bring hope to someone else. And in that moment, you will see the beauty of His design—that nothing is wasted, and that His comfort is wide enough to embrace us all.

CLOSING REFLECTION

Comfort received becomes comfort shared. In God's kingdom, even our deepest pain can be redeemed for the healing of others. May we allow His presence to soothe our hearts, and may we one day have the courage to pass that same comfort along. For the God who meets us in our grief is the same God who longs to meet others through us.

"As a mother comforts her child, so will I comfort you." (Isaiah 66:13)

PRAYER FOR THE JOURNEY

God of all comfort, thank you for meeting me in my grief
with your presence and your peace. Teach me to receive
your comfort fully, and in time, to share it with others
who are hurting. Use my story, my scars, and my sorrow
to bring hope and healing to those you place in my path.
May the comfort I offer always point back to you, the true
source of compassion and love. Amen.

CHAPTER TWENTY-TWO

Streams in the Desert

GOD'S COMFORT IS NEVER WASTED. It flows into us and through us, sustaining us when we have nothing left to give. Yet even with His comfort, there are seasons when life still feels dry and barren—when the landscape of grief looks more like a wilderness than a garden. In those moments, we cling to another promise: that God will not leave us in the desert, but will provide streams of refreshment along the way

Grief can so often feel like a desert. It is dry, barren, and empty, as though life has been stripped of color and vitality. The familiar landscape of our lives suddenly feels foreign, leaving us thirsty for comfort, for peace, for hope. In the wilderness of sorrow, every step can feel heavy, and it's easy to wonder if anything good can ever grow again.

Yet into this desert, God speaks a promise. In Isaiah 43:19, He declares: *"See, I am doing a new thing! Now it springs up; do you not perceive it? I am making a way in the wilderness and streams in the wasteland."* Even in barren places, God is at work, bringing forth life where we least expect it.

Streams in the desert don't erase the wilderness, but they transform it. They provide refreshment and renewal in the very place that once felt lifeless. In the same way, God does not deny the reality of our grief. He doesn't minimize our pain or bypass the wilderness we must walk through. But He promises to meet us there, to provide what we need to keep going, and to bring forth beauty even in barren ground.

Having experienced a traumatic loss, I will never forget those desert days of grief. They were days when my prayers felt dry, when joy felt distant, and when hope seemed like a mirage on the horizon. My heart was parched, and I wondered if I would ever feel alive again. Yet, even in that wilderness, God provided streams. Sometimes it was through His Word, a verse that spoke directly into my weary heart. Many other times it came through the quiet nudge of the Holy Spirit, bringing a line of a worship song to my mind in the middle of the night. And often, it was through small, almost hidden gifts of beauty—a beautiful morning sunrise streaking the sky with color, or the unexpected laughter of my little boy, that reminded me life still held traces of goodness. These were the streams, flowing in the desert of my sorrow, sustaining me when I felt parched.

The truth is, deserts are part of the journey. Even God's people wandered forty years through the wilderness before entering the Promised Land. But throughout their wandering, God provided water from the rock and manna from heaven. He showed them that even in barren places, His provision was certain. The same is true for us. In our grief, God does not leave us without refreshment. He provides streams, moments of His presence, that sustain us until we find our way forward.

Streams in the desert don't erase the
wilderness, but they transform it.

Life may look barren for a time, but God is always at work beneath the surface, doing something new. Healing may not come quickly, but it will come. Streams will appear where we thought only dryness could remain. And over time, what felt like wasteland can begin to blossom again—not in the same way as before, but in ways that carry new beauty, new compassion, and new hope.

When I look back, I can see that those desert days did not last forever. The landscape of grief slowly changed as God's living water began to flow. He did not remove my sorrow, but He gave me strength to endure it and moments of refreshment to remind me that I wasn't forsaken. What once felt lifeless began to carry signs of His presence, and even in my barrenness, His streams sustained me.

Scars remind us of where we've been, but God also promises refreshment for where we are going. In the barren wilderness of grief, He brings streams in the desert—unexpected moments of renewal that sustain us on the journey.

CLOSING REFLECTION

Even in the driest deserts of grief, God's streams flow. They may be quiet, small, and unexpected, but they are enough to sustain us. May we learn to look for the streams He provides—moments of beauty, whispers of hope, and reminders of His faithfulness—trusting that He is making a way where there seemed to be none.

"I will make a way in the wilderness and rivers in the desert." (Isaiah 43:19)

Lord, thank you for being the One who brings streams into my desert places. When grief leaves me dry and weary, remind me that you are near, providing refreshment for my soul. Help me to recognize the small streams of your goodness each day, and teach me to trust that you are doing a new thing, even when I cannot yet see it. Let your living water restore my spirit and bring life to the barren places of my heart. Amen.

CHAPTER TWENTY-THREE

The God Who Sees

IN THE WILDERNESS OF GRIEF, God provides streams that refresh our weary souls, reminders that He has not abandoned us. But provision is only part of the promise. Just as He brings water to barren places, He also brings His presence to lonely hearts. In the desert where we feel unseen and forgotten, He leans close and reminds us of His name—El Roi, the God who sees.

One of the loneliest parts of grief is the feeling of invisibility. The world moves on quickly, but our sorrow lingers. People may not know what to say, or they may stop asking how we are doing, assuming time has healed what time cannot touch. In those moments, it is easy to wonder if anyone truly sees the depth of our pain. Grief can make us feel like shadows—present, yet unseen.

In Genesis 16, Hagar, a woman cast out and abandoned in the desert, encounters God in her desperation. Overwhelmed and alone, she experiences His presence in such a personal way that she gives Him a new name: *El Roi,* "the God who sees me" (Genesis 16:13). She discovered in her wilderness what we long to know in ours— that God does not overlook us. He is the God who sees.

This truth is profoundly comforting as we walk through the grief journey. Our tears are not hidden. Psalm 56:8 reminds us, *"You keep track of all my sorrows. You have collected all my tears in your bottle. You have recorded each one in your book."* Every tear we cry is noticed. Every sigh is heard. Every unspoken ache is understood. God's seeing is not passive—it is deeply personal and full of compassion.

When others may forget or fail to understand, He remains near, watching over us with unwavering care.

To be seen by God means more than simply being observed. It means being known, valued, and loved in the midst of our pain. His gaze is not distant or detached; it is the attentive look of a Shepherd who knows each of His sheep by name. When others may forget or fail to understand, He remains near, watching over us with unwavering care.

I can recall seasons when I felt invisible in my grief. Friends who once checked in grew silent and distant. Many others slipped away without a word never to be heard from again. Life around me seemed to return to normal while mine felt forever altered. Yet in those moments of loneliness, God found ways to remind me that I was not forgotten. One time I was reading the Bible when all of a sudden, a verse seemed to leap off the page as though it was written just for me. Then there were all the times when a worship song would play on our Alexa and it seemed to speak directly to my heart. Oh, there were other moments when a dear friend would call or a note would arrive in the mail at the exact time I needed it most. My friends, these moments were not coincidences—they were reminders that El Roi still sees. He sees me, and He sees you!

When we know that God sees us, it changes the wilderness. The desert may not disappear, but it no longer feels abandoned. Being seen by God also means that our pain is not meaningless. He does not turn His eyes away from our sorrow but enters into it with us. His seeing is an act of love that assures us we are not walking through the valley alone. Like Hagar, we can look up through our tears and know that in the very place we feel most abandoned, God is present.

Even Jesus, during His ministry, embodied this truth. He saw the overlooked—the woman at the well, the blind man on the roadside, the children dismissed by many others. His eyes sought out those who felt invisible to the world. To be seen by Christ was to be restored to dignity and hope. And today, He still sees us with that same compassion.

When grief whispers that we are invisible, God's Word declares the opposite: we are fully seen, fully known, and fully loved. El Roi is watching over us, and His presence is our greatest comfort. He does not just see the outward expression of our grief, but the hidden aches no one else notices. And in His seeing, He meets us with care, reminding us that He is always with us.

CLOSING REFLECTION

In grief's silence, when it feels as though no one notices our pain, we can rest in this truth: God sees us. He knows every tear, every ache, every prayer too heavy to speak. May we take comfort in El Roi, the God who sees—not with judgment, but with compassion. His gaze is steady, His love unshaken, and His presence our assurance that we are never invisible to Him.

"You are the God who sees me." (Genesis 16:13)

PRAYER FOR THE JOURNEY

El Roi, the God who sees me, thank you for noticing my pain when I feel invisible. Remind me that every tear matters to you and that none of my sorrow is hidden from your gaze. Help me rest in the assurance that I am fully known and fully loved, even in my wilderness. Let your compassionate presence comfort me today and every day. Amen.

CHAPTER TWENTY-FOUR

Hope That Anchors the Soul

GRIEF OFTEN FEELS LIKE BEING tossed on stormy seas. One moment we find a little calm, and the next we are overwhelmed by waves of sorrow that seem to come out of nowhere. The steady rhythms of life we once knew are gone, and in their place, we feel adrift—unmoored, uncertain, and vulnerable to every gust of emotion. In such seasons, it can feel as though nothing is stable. But Scripture gives us this powerful reminder: *"We have this hope as an anchor for the soul, firm and secure"* (Hebrews 6:19).

An anchor does not still the storm, but it holds the vessel steady in the midst of it. In grief, hope functions in the same way. It does not erase our sorrow or prevent the winds of pain from blowing, but it grounds us in truth that is stronger than our emotions. It assures us that while life may feel unpredictable, God's promises remain unshakable.

This hope is not mere wishful thinking. It is not fragile optimism that things will get better with time. Biblical hope is confident expectation rooted in the character of God. It is knowing that His Word is true, His love is steadfast, and His presence is constant. It is trusting that He will one day make all things new, even when today feels unbearably broken.

> We may be shaken, but we are not undone.
> We may bend under the storm, but we
> are not broken beyond repair. The anchor
> holds, not because of our strength, but
> because of His.

For me, hope has often looked like clinging to God's promises when nothing else made sense. It was hope that whispered I would see my beautiful girl because of the resurrection of Christ. It was hope that reminded me my story was not finished, even when I felt stuck in sorrow. It was hope that pointed my eyes toward eternity, where every tear will be wiped away and death will be no more. These truths did not take away my grief, but they steadied me, giving me something firm to hold onto when everything else felt uncertain.

Hope as an anchor also keeps us from drifting too far into despair. Without it, sorrow can sweep us into bitterness, isolation, or hopelessness. But with hope, we are tethered to the heart of God. We may be shaken, but we are not undone. We may bend under the storm, but we are not broken beyond repair. The anchor holds, not because of our strength, but because of His.

I think of the disciples caught in the storm on the Sea of Galilee. As waves crashed around them, they panicked, forgetting that Jesus was in the boat. He rose and calmed the storm with a word, but the deeper lesson was clear: even when the winds howl and the water rages, His presence is the anchor that secures us. In grief, we too forget at times that Christ is in our boat. Yet He remains, steady and unshaken, holding us fast when we feel like we're drowning.

Storms will come, and grief will ebb and flow. But no storm can sever the anchor of hope we have in Christ. His promises are unchanging, His love is unfailing, and His resurrection guarantees that death does not have the final word. When waves of sorrow rise, we can rest in this truth: the anchor holds, and it will hold us fast until the day He brings us safely home.

CLOSING REFLECTION

Grief may toss us like waves on a restless sea, but our hope in Christ is the anchor that holds us secure. This hope is not fragile—it is firm, rooted in His promises and guaranteed by His resurrection. When despair tempts us to drift, may we cling to the anchor of His love, trusting that no storm can pull us from His grasp.

"We have this hope as an anchor for the soul, firm and secure." (Hebrews 6:19)

PRAYER FOR THE JOURNEY

Lord, thank you for being the anchor of my soul when grief makes me feel adrift. Remind me that my hope is not in changing circumstances, but in your unchanging promises. When the storms of sorrow rise, keep me steady in your love. Help me cling to the assurance of eternity and the certainty of your presence, until the day when every tear is wiped away and I am forever secure in you. Amen.

CHAPTER TWENTY-FIVE

When Darkness Turns to Dawn

So OFTEN AS WE VENTURE down this road we didn't choose to be on, grief can feel like an endless night. The world around us may continue to turn, but inside, it is dark, heavy, and quiet in a way that feels unbearable. Nights of grief are long and so hard to endure; hours can stretch on endlessly when sleep refuses to come and sorrow presses in on every side. Even when the sun rises outside, it can feel as though our hearts remain cloaked in shadow.

The psalmist gives us this promise: *"Weeping may last through the night, but joy comes with the morning"* (Psalm 30:5). This verse doesn't deny the night. It acknowledges the tears, the weariness, the pain. But it also points us toward hope that the night will not last forever. Morning will come. Light will break through.

Let me encourage here for a moment. During those long, hard, and lonely nights, just hold on. Take it one moment, and even one breath at a time. Why? Because dawn is one of God's most tender reminders that darkness is not permanent. Slowly, almost imperceptibly at first, the blackness of night gives way to shades of gray, then soft hues of pink, orange, and gold. It is never sudden; it is gradual, steady, and sure. In the same way, healing from grief often comes quietly, step by step. It doesn't erase the night, but it assures us that sorrow will not always be forever.

The tears we cry in the dark become the
backdrop against which the light shines
brighter.

I can recall the moments when light first began breaking through my own night of grief. At first, it was subtle—a memory of my daughter that now brought warmth instead of only tears, a day when laughter returned in small but meaningful ways. These were glimpses of dawn, reminders that while the night of sorrow was real, it would not last forever. The darkness didn't completely disappear, but it no longer held the same power.

Isaiah 9:2 says, *"The people walking in darkness have seen a great light; on those living in the land of deep darkness a light has dawned."* That light is Christ Himself. He enters into our night not only to comfort us but to bring us through it. He is the assurance that morning will come. His resurrection is the ultimate dawn, proof that even death itself cannot hold back the light of His love.

For those still in the thick of grief, dawn may feel far away and unattainable. The hours of sorrow can stretch on unbearably, and the thought of joy can feel out of reach. But even when we cannot see it, don't give up—the light is coming. Just as the sun never fails to rise, God's faithfulness never fails to reach us. It may come gently, in ways we hardly notice at first, but it will come. His mercies are new every morning, and each sunrise is a reminder that His promises still stand.

It is important to remember that the dawn does not erase the night—it follows it. The depth of our mourning makes the arrival of joy all the more profound. The tears we cry in the dark become the backdrop against which the light shines brighter. Just as the disciples' despair on Friday made the joy of resurrection Sunday so much greater, so too does our grief make the hope of Christ's light more powerful.

The night of grief may be long, but it is not endless. One day, whether here in glimpses of healing or in eternity when all sorrow is gone, the light will break through fully. Until then, we hold onto the hope of morning, trusting that the same God who keeps the stars in place will also bring the dawn to our weary hearts.

CLOSING REFLECTION

Grief's night may linger, but it cannot last forever. The promise of dawn is sure, because Christ Himself is our light. Each sunrise whispers of His mercy, each glimpse of laughter or peace points to His faithfulness. May we hold fast to this hope: the night will end, the morning will come, and the Light of the world will never leave us in the dark.

"The people walking in darkness have seen a great light; on those living in the land of deep darkness a light has dawned." (Isaiah 9:2)

PRAYER FOR THE JOURNEY

Lord, thank you for the promise that the night of sorrow will not last forever. When grief feels like endless darkness, remind me that your mercies are new every morning. Teach me to look for the glimpses of light you send, and to trust that joy will come again in your time. Be my dawn, Lord, and bring your healing light into the darkest places of my heart. Amen.

CHAPTER TWENTY-SIX

New Mercies Every Morning

DAWN REMINDS US THAT DARKNESS will not last forever, but with each sunrise comes another gift—new mercies for the day ahead. The same God who promises that joy will come in the morning also assures us that His compassion never runs dry. Each day is met with fresh grace, perfectly measured for what we need. And so, as the light breaks through, we discover not only the hope of dawn but the steady provision of new mercies each morning.

When we are in the deep of it, grief has a way of making the future feel impossible. When the weight of loss presses down, even the thought of tomorrow can be overwhelming. We may find ourselves asking, *How will I survive the days, months, or years ahead without the one I love?* The emptiness ahead seem too vast to face. In those moments, God gently reminds us that He does not ask us to live tomorrow today. He gives us strength for this day, and with each new morning, He will give new strength again.

Lamentations 3:22–23 offers this promise: *"Because of the Lord's great love we are not consumed, for his compassions never fail. They are new every morning; great is your faithfulness."* These words were written in the midst of deep suffering. Jeremiah, the prophet, was mourning the destruction of Jerusalem, surrounded by grief and despair. Yet even in that devastation, he declared hope: God's mercies are new every morning.

We don't have to know how we will endure every painful milestone or unexpected wave of sorrow that resurfaces in the months and years to come. We only need to trust that when those days arrive, God's mercy will meet us there.

This truth is a lifeline for the grieving heart. God's compassion is not given to us in bulk for a lifetime—it is poured out fresh each day. Yesterday's sorrow does not deplete today's mercy. Tomorrow's worries do not diminish the strength He provides for today. Each morning, as the sun rises, so does His faithful love, giving us what we need for the day before us.

I will never forget the crushing heaviness my heart felt at the idea of facing the future without my only daughter. Thinking ahead only magnified the ache in my heart. How would I endure birthdays, anniversaries, or holidays without her? But God taught me to live one day at a time. He reminded me that His mercy was not about carrying the weight of an entire lifetime of grief at once, but about sustaining me moment by moment. Some days, that mercy looked like the courage to get out of bed. Other days, it looked like the strength to laugh again without guilt. Always, it was enough for that day.

Living in this truth frees us from the burden of trying to figure out the entire journey of grief. We don't have to know how we will endure every painful milestone or unexpected wave of sorrow that resurfaces in the months and years to come. We only need to trust that when those days arrive, God's mercy will meet us there, just as it meets us now. His faithfulness does not run out. His compassion does not fail.

Every sunrise is a sermon in the sky—a reminder that God hasn't forgotten us. His mercies are as sure as the dawn, as steady as the turning of the earth. Even when we wake to a heart that still aches, we can also wake to the assurance that His love will carry us through this day. And when tomorrow comes, He will be there again with new mercy, just as He promised.

Perhaps this is why Jesus said, *"Do not worry about tomorrow, for tomorrow will worry about itself. Each day has enough trouble of its own"* (Matthew 6:34). The call is not to minimize our grief but to lean on God's grace for the present moment. We cannot stockpile tomorrow's mercy in advance, but we can rest in the certainty that it will be waiting for us when we need it.

The rhythm of sunrise and sunset becomes holy in its reminder: God's compassion comes with the dawn. Just as He provided manna daily for His people in the wilderness, He provides daily mercies for us in the wilderness of grief. Not too much, not too little—just what we need for each day.

CLOSING REFLECTION

God's mercies rise with the morning sun. They are new, steady, and perfectly suited for the day ahead. May we rest in the truth that we do not walk into an unknown future alone, but with a God whose compassions never fail. Let every sunrise remind us that His love is faithful, His grace sufficient, and His mercy more than enough for today.

"They are new every morning; great is Your faithfulness." (Lamentations 3:23)

PRAYER FOR THE JOURNEY

Lord, thank you that your mercies are new every morning.
When grief makes the future feel overwhelming, help me
to rest in the strength you provide for today. Teach me to
take one step at a time, trusting that tomorrow will hold
its own portion of your grace. Great is your faithfulness,
Lord, and I place my hope in your steadfast love. Amen

CHAPTER TWENTY-SEVEN

When Joy Returns

THERE'S A TENDER TRUTH ABOUT grief that often feels impossible to believe in the beginning: joy will return. In the early days of loss, that promise can feel distant, even unthinkable. When your world has been shattered, when silence feels deafening, and when every breath hurts, the idea of joy can feel like a betrayal of your grief. But slowly, gently, it begins to reappear. It won't look exactly the same as it did before your loss, and it may arrive in fleeting, fragile moments at first. But it will come.

In my early days after losing Melanie, the thought of feeling joy about anything in life seemed almost wrong. How could I smile when my heart was so shattered? How could I enjoy a moment without feeling like I was betraying her memory? For a long time, the weight of guilt pressed against every flicker of joy, silencing laughter before it could rise. Yet over time, I discovered that joy doesn't replace grief—it grows alongside it. And when it does, it brings a kind of beauty and depth I had never known before.

Joy began to slip back into my life quietly, almost unnoticed at first. It came in a friend's unexpected visit and in the sound of my other children's laughter. At first, those moments felt delicate, as if they might shatter under the weight of my sorrow. I would catch myself smiling, then quickly wonder if it was too soon. But joy has a way of gently pushing past our resistance. Slowly, it became more frequent, more natural, reminding me that love and loss are not enemies but companions. I also knew deep in my heart that Melanie would not want me to get lost and forever weighed down in my grief, but instead live with joy and happiness.

Here's what I've learned: joy is not a denial of your loss—it is evidence that love has left its mark so deeply that life still has meaning, even in the shadow of grief. It doesn't erase sorrow, but it brings balance to it. Joy and grief can sit side by side, reminding us that even in our pain, there is still goodness to be seen, laughter to be heard, and beauty to be found.

There will always be days when grief feels heavier, when memories ache more sharply, and when the valley seems endless. That is the nature of love woven with loss. But there will also be days when you realize you've laughed without guilt, when gratitude rises without tears, when you've lived a whole day and found yourself whispering, "Thank You, Lord, for this gift."

When joy returns, embrace it. Allow it to remind you that your story isn't only about loss—it's also about life, resilience, and hope. Joy does not diminish your love for the one who is gone. If anything, it deepens it, showing that their life continues to shape you in ways that bring light into the world. To smile again, to laugh again, to feel the warmth of joy again, is not to forget—it is to carry forward the love that remains.

Joy is not a denial of your loss—it is evidence that love has left its mark so deeply that life still has meaning, even in the shadow of grief. It doesn't erase sorrow, but it brings balance to it.

Joy is a sign of God's faithfulness, a reminder that He has not abandoned you in the dark valley. Like the first rays of dawn breaking through a long night, joy is His way of whispering that life, though forever changed, is still worth living. And as you continue the journey, you will see that grief and joy, hand in hand, can tell a story of love, healing, and endurance that only God could write.

CLOSING REFLECTION

The return of joy does not mean the absence of grief - it means that God is gently teaching our hearts to hold both at once. Every smile, every laugh, every moment of gratitude is a testimony that love is stronger than loss and that God's promises are true. When joy returns, receive it as a gift, not with guilt but with gratitude. For it is the Shepherd Himself who restores our souls, reminding us that even after nights of weeping, morning will come.

"You turned my wailing into dancing; you removed my sackcloth and clothed me with joy." (Psalm 30:11)

PRAYER FOR THE JOURNEY

Lord, thank you for the moments when joy returns to my weary heart. Help me to receive them without guilt, knowing they are your gifts of healing. Remind me that joy does not erase my love for the one I miss, but honors it. May I live with open hands, ready to receive every good thing you still have for me. Amen.

PART SIX

Community and Compassion

CHAPTER TWENTY-EIGHT

Ways We Can Honor Our Loved Ones

As each anniversary of a loved one's passing approaches, we may find ourselves overwhelmed by a mix of emotions and memories. These days can be bittersweet. On one hand they can be filled with the joy of remembrance, yet on the other hand, they can be heavy with the ache of absence. The pain of loss often rises to the surface again, reminding us of the depth of our love. Missing someone who meant so much to us is a natural and healthy part of grief. But learning how to navigate these tender moments can help us honor their memory while caring for our own hearts. While there are many ways we can honor our loved ones, these are just a few thoughts:

ACKNOWLEDGE YOUR FEELINGS

The first step toward healing is giving yourself permission to feel. Grief doesn't follow a schedule, and anniversaries can reopen wounds no matter how many years have passed. You might experience sadness, anger, guilt, or loneliness. Allow yourself to feel without judgment. These emotions are reminders of the love you still carry.

By acknowledging our emotions, leaning
on others, and finding personal ways to
celebrate their life, we transform grief into
a lasting tribute of love.

CREATE A MEANINGFUL RITUAL

Consider establishing a tradition that feels personal and honoring. This could mean visiting their grave, lighting a candle, preparing their favorite meal, sending lanterns or balloons up into the night sky, or simply spending time in a place they loved. Looking through old photographs or writing them a letter can also bring comfort. Rituals not only preserve memories but also create intentional space for connection.

REACH OUT FOR SUPPORT

Grief can feel isolating, but you do not have to walk through it alone. Lean on trusted friends, family, or grief support groups. Share stories, talk about your emotions, or simply sit with someone who understands. Sometimes, the greatest comfort comes from knowing others remember your loved one too.

LEAN ON YOUR FAITH

If you hold spiritual beliefs, draw strength from them. Prayer, meditation, or reading scripture can anchor you during emotional waves. Reflect on the hope of eternal life or the enduring impact of your loved one's legacy. Faith can help turn sorrow into gratitude for the time you shared.

BE GENTLE WITH YOURSELF

Give yourself grace. There is no right or wrong way to grieve, or any specific way you should feel on an anniversary. Allow space for both tears and joy, for solitude and companionship. Your love didn't end when they passed—it lives on in you.

While anniversaries of loss can be painful, they can also become sacred opportunities to remember, honor, and continue loving. By acknowledging our emotions, leaning on others, and finding personal ways to celebrate their life, we transform grief into a lasting tribute of love.

CLOSING REFLECTION

To honor our loved ones is to carry their light forward. Every story shared, every tradition continued, every act of kindness in their name keeps their legacy alive. Though grief reminds us of what we've lost, love reminds us of what endures.

"The memory of the righteous is a blessing" (Proverbs 10:7).

PRAYER FOR THE JOURNEY

Father, I bring my heart before you. Thank you for the gift of my loved one's life and for every moment we shared. Comfort me in the waves of sorrow, and help me find peace in your presence. Give me the strength to honor their memory with love, hope, and grace. May my heart rest in the promise that we will meet again in your eternal home. Amen.

CHAPTER TWENTY-NINE

Words of Comfort

FOR THOSE WHO HAVE LOST a loved one, memories often surface of well-meaning friends who stopped by to offer condolences, hoping to bring comfort in the midst of sorrow. Their hearts were in the right place, but sometimes the words spoken had the opposite effect of what they intended. Grief is such a fragile, tender place, and words, no matter how kindly meant, can land with surprising sharpness. Even the smallest phrases can pierce a grieving heart if not spoken with care.

The truth is, each of us will encounter grief at some point in our lives. For some, it comes in the form of personal loss. For others, it may mean walking closely beside a friend or family member who is hurting. In those sacred and sorrow-filled spaces, our desire to help is genuine. We want to ease the burden, to say something that will make the pain lighter. And yet, so often, our words can miss the mark.

I remember after my daughter passed away, a friend gently remarked, *"Thankfully, you have two other children."* I knew this came from a sincere place, an attempt to remind me of the blessings that still surrounded me. But those words, though meant to comfort, diminished the irreplaceable loss I had suffered. No child could ever replace another. Each life is unique, each relationship sacred, and the absence of one leaves a void that nothing and no one else can fill.

What grievers often need most is not advice but presence. It's the steady assurance that someone is there, ready to listen, willing to sit in silence, unafraid of tears.

In the face of deep grief, there are no magic words to mend a broken heart. But there are ways to bring true comfort if we allow ourselves to lean into empathy rather than rushing toward solutions. Sometimes the most healing words are the simplest acknowledgments: *"I'm so sorry for your loss."* Or, *"I can't imagine how hard this is for you."* Even a quiet, *"There are no words,"* can bring more solace than a well-rehearsed phrase. Such expressions honor the depth of sorrow without attempting to fix what cannot be fixed.

What grievers often need most is not advice but presence. It's the steady assurance that someone is there, ready to listen, willing to sit in silence, unafraid of tears. When friends allowed me to speak Melanie's name, to share stories I had already told a dozen times, I felt the tender gift of being understood. Their willingness to listen—without rushing me past my pain—was far more valuable than any polished sentence could ever be.

On the other hand, there are phrases that can wound deeply, even if unintentional. "At least..." statements often dismiss the rawness of grief by pushing silver linings too soon: *"At least she's in a better place."* *"At least you had her for the years you did."* These words may come from good intentions, but they minimize the depth of the loss and the immensity of love that remains. Comparisons to other losses can sting as well, as each grief journey is as unique as the relationship itself. What comforted one person may not comfort another.

When in doubt, it is always safer to listen. To extend compassion through presence. To remember that sometimes the quiet companionship of a friend speaks louder than any words could. Silence, paired with a hand held, a hug offered, or a listening ear, communicates more love than any tidy phrase ever could.

When comfort feels hard to give, let empathy be the guide. Grief calls for gentleness, patience, and a willingness to stand alongside the hurting without rushing them forward. In those moments, our presence becomes the truest gift we can offer—a living reflection of God's tender heart.

Paul reminds us of this sacred calling in Romans 12:15: *"Rejoice with those who rejoice; mourn with those who mourn."* To comfort is not to erase sorrow but to share in it. It is to step into another's valley, acknowledging the weight they carry, and offering love that listens more than it speaks.

CLOSING REFLECTION

True comfort is not found in perfect words but in faithful presence. To sit with the grieving, to listen without judgment, to weep alongside them—this is where love becomes tangible. Words may falter, but compassion never fails. And as we comfort others with gentleness, we become the hands and feet of Christ, who is Himself the God of all comfort.

"Praise be to the God... who comforts us in all our troubles, so that we can comfort those in any trouble with the comfort we ourselves receive from God." (2 Corinthians 1:3–4)

PRAYER FOR THE JOURNEY

Father, teach us to be gentle with our words and generous with our presence. Help us listen with compassion and love without rushing to fix. May we honor the pain of those who grieve by acknowledging their loss, standing beside them, and reflecting your tender heart. Lord, let our words—and even our silences—be vessels of your comfort. Amen.

CHAPTER THIRTY

Receiving Comfort in Grief

COMFORT IS NEVER JUST ONE-SIDED. While it matters deeply how we extend compassion to others, there is also a holy vulnerability in learning how to receive it ourselves. Allowing someone to step into our pain is not weakness—it is courage.

If offering comfort to the grieving requires tenderness and care, receiving comfort can be just as delicate a journey. It requires trust. When we find ourselves in the depths of loss, it can feel unnatural, even impossible, to let others into our pain. Grief has a way of isolating us. It whispers that no one else can understand, that to invite others in might somehow diminish the sacredness of our sorrow. Yet one of the hardest truths to accept is also one of the most freeing: we were never meant to carry grief alone.

After my daughter's death, I remember moments when friends and family reached out with open hands and willing hearts, only for me to hesitate. My instinct was to retreat into solitude, to curl tightly around the ache of loss. It felt safer to sit with my pain than to risk hearing words that might cut deeper. But slowly, God began to show me that receiving comfort is not weakness. It is an act of courage, a humble recognition that we need one another.

Allowing others to enter our grief is a way of honoring both our pain and their love. When someone shows up to sit beside us, they are offering a piece of themselves—time, energy, and heart. Saying yes to their presence is not a burden to them; it's an invitation to relationship. It doesn't mean that their presence will take away the sorrow. It means that we don't have to face the weight of it in isolation.

Still, receiving comfort requires patience, because not everyone will know the right thing to say or do. There will be awkward moments and clumsy words. I've had people say things that unintentionally hurt more than helped. Yet instead of closing off, I've learned to let grace cover the missteps. Sometimes what mattered most wasn't whether someone said the perfect thing—it was that they cared enough to say anything at all, to risk stepping into my pain even when it was uncomfortable.

There is a holy humility in letting others see our tears. In a world that often prizes strength and composure, allowing someone to witness our rawness feels vulnerable, even frightening. Yet those moments of vulnerability create sacred space. When we allow others to hear the story of our loved one, to speak their name, or to sit quietly with us, we give them a gift too: the chance to participate in the sacred work of remembrance. Our grief becomes shared rather than hidden, and in that sharing, we discover a strength that solitude cannot provide.

Receiving comfort is, at its heart, an act of trust. We trust that God will send the right people at the right time. We trust that His Spirit can speak through imperfect words and stumbling gestures. And we trust that by opening our hearts, even just a little, we create space for healing to take root.

Allowing others to enter our grief is a way
of honoring both our pain and their love.

Jesus Himself modeled this when He allowed Mary and Martha to grieve openly before Him at Lazarus's tomb. He didn't tell them to hide their sorrow or to handle it on their own. He entered into their pain, weeping with them before performing the miracle. That moment reminds us that if even the Son of God welcomed and shared in human grief, we too can allow others to draw near to us in our sorrow.

In truth, receiving comfort is not only about us—it is also about community. When we let others in, we remind them that grief is not something to fear or avoid. We show them that love is strong enough to hold both tears and silence. And in turn, they may one day be better prepared to walk with someone else who is grieving, carrying forward the legacy of compassion that began with our willingness to receive.

For those who grieve, we will often feel uncomfortable being vulnerable and transparent, allowing others to witness our pain. But the healing journey is not meant to be traveled in solitude. When we welcome others into our sorrow, we mirror the very heart of God, who comforts us so that we might comfort one another.

CLOSING REFLECTION

To receive comfort is to admit that we cannot walk this journey alone—and that is not a weakness, but a gift. When we open our hearts to the love of others, we also open ourselves more fully to the love of God, who often sends His compassion through the people around us. Grief may tempt us to isolate, but healing grows best in the soil of community. Let us be willing not only to give comfort but also to receive it, trusting that the God of all compassion will meet us there.

"Carry each other's burdens, and in this way you will fulfill the law of Christ." (Galatians 6:2)

Lord, help me to open my heart to the comfort you send through others. Teach me to receive love without fear, to accept presence without feeling like a burden. Give me the grace to embrace imperfect words and to recognize the tenderness behind them. May I learn to let others walk with me, even in my pain, and may your Spirit use their love as a balm for my soul. Amen.

CHAPTER THIRTY-ONE

The Ministry of Presence

WHEN WORDS FAIL, AND THEY often do in times of grief, presence becomes the language of love. We may think that comfort must always be spoken, that the right phrase will ease the ache of loss, but more often than not, it is simply showing up that matters most. The ministry of presence is one of the greatest gifts we can offer or receive, for it communicates something words never could: *you are not alone.*

When Melanie died, there were countless moments when conversations felt impossible. No words could mend the fracture in my heart, and no explanation could make sense of what had happened. Yet I remember with deep gratitude those who came and sat with me in silence. They didn't come with answers, nor did they try to fill the space with chatter. Their presence itself spoke volumes. In their quiet companionship, I felt the nearness of God, tangible, steady, and unshakable.

The ministry of presence mirrors the heart of Christ. When Mary and Martha lost their brother Lazarus, Scripture tells us that Jesus wept alongside them (John 11:35). The Son of God, who had the power to raise the dead, chose first to share their sorrow. He did not immediately rush to the miracle but paused to enter into their grief. In that simple act of weeping with them, He revealed the depth of His compassion and the sacredness of presence.

The ministry of presence is one of the
greatest gifts we can offer or receive, for
it communicates something words never
could: you are not alone.

Being present doesn't require eloquence, wisdom, or even answers. It requires availability. It means setting aside our need to fix or explain and instead choosing to sit in the discomfort of another's pain. Presence says, *"I see you. I grieve with you. I will not leave you alone in this valley."* It transforms loneliness into companionship, and in that companionship, hearts can begin to breathe again.

Of course, the ministry of presence is not always easy. It can feel uncomfortable and awkward to sit in silence, to resist the urge to fill the air with words. We fear we might say the wrong thing or worry that our quiet presence isn't enough. But in truth, presence is often the very thing a grieving heart longs for most. A hand held in silence, a shoulder offered for tears, or simply sitting side by side can speak louder than a thousand carefully chosen words.

Presence also requires sacrifice. To show up for someone in grief means putting aside our schedules, our convenience, and sometimes even our comfort. It means entering into the sacred space of another's pain and choosing to remain there, even when it feels heavy. But it is in those moments that love becomes most visible. Just as Christ entered into our humanity, bearing our burdens, we too are called to bear one another's burdens (Galatians 6:2).

For those walking through grief, the willingness of others to show up, even without answers, is a reminder of God's faithfulness. He often uses human companionship to reflect His own steadfast love. Each person who enters into our pain with quiet courage becomes a vessel of His comfort, carrying His light into the darkest of valleys.

And yet, presence is not only a gift given to others, it is also one we must be willing to receive. To allow someone to sit with us in our grief, to let them see our tears and hear our silence, is itself an act of trust. It is a reminder that God never intended for us to carry our burdens alone. When we welcome the presence of others, we also open our hearts to the presence of God, who promises never to leave us nor forsake us.

The ministry of presence also teaches us that we don't need to do extraordinary things to make a difference. Sometimes, the most extraordinary act is simply to be there. And in that simplicity, healing begins to take root. Presence may not remove the pain, but it lessens the loneliness, and in that shared space, hope quietly begins to stir.

CLOSING REFLECTION

The ministry of presence is the echo of Christ's love through human hands and hearts. When we sit with the grieving, we carry His compassion into their sorrow. When we allow others to sit with us, we receive the gift of His nearness through them. Words may falter, but presence never fails, because it reflects the eternal promise of Emmanuel—God with us.

"Never will I leave you; never will I forsake you." (Hebrews 13:5)

PRAYER FOR THE JOURNEY

Lord, thank you for the gift of presence. Teach us to show up for others with quiet courage and open hearts. Help us resist the urge to fix or explain, and instead reflect your compassion through our companionship. When words fail, may our silence carry your love. And when we are the ones grieving, give us the humility to receive the gift of presence from others, knowing it is you working through them. Amen.

CHAPTER THIRTY-TWO

Carrying One Another's Burdens

CAN WE ALL AGREE THAT grief is heavy? It presses down on the heart, clouds the mind, and weakens the body. In the midst of deep loss, even the smallest tasks, like cooking a meal, answering the phone, or getting out of bed can feel overwhelming. Yet God, in His wisdom, designed us not to carry such weight alone. Scripture reminds us in Galatians 6:2, *"Carry each other's burdens, and in this way, you will fulfill the law of Christ."*

There is something profoundly healing about knowing others are willing to step in and shoulder part of what feels unbearable. Sometimes this looks like physical help: meals delivered to the doorstep, rides given, or errands quietly taken care of without fanfare. Other times, it looks like emotional and spiritual support: a friend who prays faithfully, someone who checks in with a simple text, or the one who consistently shows up even months after the funeral has passed. Each act, whether large or small, becomes a thread in the fabric of love that surrounds a grieving heart.

I remember the tender kindness of friends who stepped into my pain when I could not take another step on my own. Friends set up a meal train and meals miraculously showed up on our doorstep night after night, ensuring my family was fed when I had no energy to cook. These seemingly ordinary gestures carried a sacred weight.

The truth is, when we carry one another's burdens, we are reflecting Christ Himself. Jesus bore the ultimate burden at the cross, carrying not only the weight of sin but also the depth of human sorrow. He knows our pain intimately, and through His people, He extends His comfort. When we offer a hand, a prayer, or even a listening ear, we are participating in His ministry of compassion.

Carrying burdens doesn't mean we take away someone's grief—no human hand has the power to erase such loss. Instead, it means we choose to walk alongside, helping to ease the load, even if only slightly. It is the ministry of saying, *"I will stand here with you. I will help carry what I can, for as long as it takes."* That kind of faithful love reminds the grieving that they are held not only by God but also by a community of His people who embody His care.

For those who are grieving, allowing others to carry some of the weight can feel difficult. Pride, guilt, or if you're anything like me and think you're Wonder Woman who can handle everything all by yourself—the instinct to retreat into solitude may tempt us to push help away. We may feel that accepting help is a burden to others, or we may fear that our vulnerability is too raw to be seen. Yet part of healing comes in saying yes—yes to the meal, yes to the prayer, yes to the presence of others. In doing so, we give others the opportunity to live out the love of Christ in tangible ways, and we open ourselves to the blessing of community.

There is also a quiet reciprocity in this truth. The one who carries today may be the one in need of carrying tomorrow. Burden-bearing is not a one-time act, but a rhythm of community that reflects God's design for His people. In Romans 12:15, Paul reminds us to *"mourn with those who mourn."* This shared journey of grief binds us together in a way that is both humbling and holy.

There is something profoundly healing about knowing others are willing to step in and shoulder part of what feels unbearable.

In the end, carrying one another's burdens is not about grand gestures but about faithful love. It is the simple yet sacred act of lightening the load for a weary soul, one small step at a time. And in those moments, the heart of Christ is revealed.

CLOSING REFLECTION

Carrying one another's burdens is a sacred calling, both to give and to receive. When we show up in love, we reflect the compassion of Christ. When we allow others to enter our pain, we open the door for healing to take root. Grief is too heavy for one person to bear alone, but in the fellowship of believers, no one has to. May we be willing to carry and to be carried, trusting that through each act of love, God Himself is present.

"Therefore encourage one another and build each other up, just as in fact you are doing." (1 Thessalonians 5:11)

PRAYER FOR THE JOURNEY

Lord, thank you for calling us into community, where no one has to carry their grief alone. Teach us to notice the burdens others are carrying and to step in with love, compassion, and grace. Give us the courage to accept help when we are the ones in need, knowing that you work through the hands and hearts of others. May we always reflect your love by bearing one another's burdens, just as you bore ours. Amen.

PART SEVEN

Hope Rising in the Storm

CHAPTER THIRTY-THREE

The Healing Power of Hope

I'VE OFTEN THOUGHT THAT GRIEF can feel like a heavy shadow that refuses to lift. When the journey first began, it may seem impossible to imagine a future where happiness could exist again. Every breath feels weighted, every step exhausting. Yet even in the deepest valleys, God plants something that has the power to keep us moving forward: hope.

Hope is not denial of our pain, nor is it a shallow optimism that ignores reality. True hope is rooted in the promises of God, promises that don't shift with our circumstances. It is the steady assurance that this sorrow is not the end of our story. Paul writes in 1 Thessalonians 4:13, *"And now, dear brothers and sisters, we want you to know what will happen to the believers who have died so you will not grieve like people who have no hope."* Notice he doesn't say we will not grieve. He acknowledges that grief is inevitable, but he reminds us that as children of God, our grief is infused with the hope of reunion, redemption, and eternal life.

For me, hope became a lifeline in the days after my daughter's death. The ache of her absence was unbearable, yet the thought that I would one day see her again gave me strength to endure. I began to realize that hope doesn't erase grief—it gives it a new dimension.

Grief says, "I miss you." Hope whispers, "I will see you again." The two live side by side, and together they shape a path forward.

Sometimes hope appears in small, quiet ways. It shows up in the beauty of a spring morning after a sleepless night, in a gentle word from a friend, or in the strength to make it through one more day. Other times, hope feels bold and unshakable, lifting our eyes from the pain of this world to the glory of eternity. Both forms of hope are gifts. Both remind us that God has not left us in despair but has placed His promises like anchors for our souls.

Of course, there are days when hope feels far away. The darkness of grief can cloud our vision, and we may wonder if we will ever feel light again. In those moments, we are reminded that hope is not something we manufacture on our own—it is something God gives. Romans 15:13 declares, *"May the God of hope fill you with all joy and peace as you trust in him, so that you may overflow with hope by the power of the Holy Spirit."* Hope is a divine gift, poured into us by the Spirit, steadying us when we cannot steady ourselves.

The healing power of hope does not erase our tears, but it gives those tears meaning. It reminds us that love never dies, that life is stronger than death, and that God is faithful to His promises. With hope, we can take one step at a time, trusting that even in our sorrow, God is leading us toward a future filled with His presence and peace.

Hope is also what connects our earthly journey with eternity. Revelation 21:4 offers one of the most profound promises: *"He will wipe every tear from their eyes. There will be no more death or mourning or crying or pain, for the old order of things has passed away."* This is the ultimate hope—the assurance that grief itself is temporary. One day, sorrow will cease, and joy will be eternal. Holding onto this promise sustains us when today feels unbearable.

In the end, hope is not about forgetting our grief but about walking through it with the knowledge that this is not the final chapter. Grief and hope can dwell in the same heart. Grief honors the depth of our love; hope honors the depth of God's promises. Together, they carry us forward.

CLOSING REFLECTION

Hope does not take away the reality of grief, but it transforms the way we walk through it. It is the quiet voice that reminds us we are not abandoned, the steady anchor that keeps us from drifting into despair, and the radiant promise that life is not over—it is being redeemed. May we cling to the God of hope, allowing His Spirit to fill us with peace, strength, and courage for each step of the journey.

"But those who hope in the Lord will renew their strength. They will soar on wings like eagles; they will run and not grow weary; they will walk and not be faint." (Isaiah 40:31)

PRAYER FOR THE JOURNEY

God of all comfort, thank you for the gift of hope that anchors our souls in the storm of grief. When the shadows feel heavy, lift our eyes to see your promises. When despair threatens to overtake us, breathe fresh hope into our hearts. Teach us to trust that this is not the end of the story, but that eternal joy awaits in your presence. May your Spirit fill us with hope, sustaining us day by day until the day when every tear is wiped away. Amen.

CHAPTER THIRTY-FOUR

When Grief Returns Like a Tsunami

IF ONLY GRIEF FOLLOWED A straight line. If only it moved predict-ably from sorrow to healing, never circling back, never catching us off guard. But grief does not behave that way. It is not linear. It's more like the ocean, sometimes calm and still, other times crashing with relentless force, like a tsunami. Even after years have passed, grief can return, surprising us with its strength and pulling us back into places we thought we had already left behind.

There have been moments when I was doing well, when laughter was possible again, and the heaviness of loss seemed to have lifted just enough for me to breathe deeply. And then, out of nowhere, something as small as a song on the radio or the scent of a favorite food would break me open again. Tears would flow freely, and the ache in my chest would feel as raw as it did in those first days. At first, I thought this meant I was failing in my grief journey, as though I hadn't moved forward at all. But over time, I began to see these waves differently. They were not signs of weakness; they were reminders of the love that still exists for my girl.

Grief returns because love endures. The bond we shared with the one we lost doesn't vanish with time; it remains etched into our hearts. When a memory or milestone stirs the sorrow again, it is proof that the love was real, deep, and worth remembering. Just as the tides of the sea are pulled by forces unseen, so too are our hearts drawn back to the places where love and loss meet.

Grief returns because love endures. The bond we shared with the one we lost doesn't vanish with time; it remains etched into our hearts.

These waves may knock us off balance, but they can also carry us closer to God. Each surge of grief is an invitation to lean once again on His steady presence. The Psalmist writes, *"From the end of the earth I call to you, when my heart is faint. Lead me to the rock that is higher than I"* (Psalm 61:2). When the waves threaten to overwhelm, He becomes our Rock—the One who lifts us above the waters and gives us a firm place to stand.

There is a certain rhythm to grief, a pattern we eventually learn to recognize. Healing does not mean the absence of waves; it means finding our balance in their midst. Some days the sea will be gentle, and you'll find space to breathe, to laugh, to live fully. Other days it will feel wild and unrelenting, pulling you back into sorrow you thought had quieted. Both are part of the journey. Both are part of love's enduring story.

I have come to see these waves as holy reminders. They remind me that my daughter's life was woven so deeply into mine that her absence will always be felt. They remind me that grief is not about erasing her memory but about honoring her place in my heart. And they remind me that God's presence is as constant as the tides, always there, always steady, even when my emotions rise and fall.

When grief returns like the fiercest waves, it is not regression. It is not failure. It is simply love resurfacing, calling us to remember, to weep, and to lean once more on the Shepherd who never lets us drown. Scripture assures us of this promise: *"When you pass through the waters, I will be with you; and when you pass through the rivers, they will not sweep over you"* (Isaiah 43:2). We may feel the force of the waves, but we are never abandoned in them.

So, when the tide of grief rises unexpectedly, let it come. Let the tears fall. Let the memories surface. And then, rest in the truth that the God who commands the seas is the same God who holds your heart. The waves may return, but so will His presence—faithful, steady, and strong enough to carry you through.

CLOSING REFLECTION

Grief is not a straight road but a shoreline, where waves rise and fall with the rhythm of love and memory. When the waters return, let them remind you that your love is still alive, and your story is still unfolding in God's hands. The One who calms the seas also steadies your heart, teaching you to breathe again even when the tide is strong.

"He reached down from on high and took hold of me; he drew me out of deep waters." (Psalm 18:16)

PRAYER FOR THE JOURNEY

Lord, when the waves of grief crash over me, steady my heart and remind me that sorrow is not a sign of weakness but of love that still lives within me. Help me to see your hand holding me above the waters, guiding me to rest in you. Teach me to trust that every wave brings me closer to your presence and to the day when you will calm every storm. Amen.

CHAPTER THIRTY-FIVE

Faith in the Valley

FAITH IS OFTEN CELEBRATED ON the mountaintops of life—those seasons when blessings overflow, prayers are answered, and joy comes easily. But faith takes on a different shape in the valley, where shadows stretch long and sorrow settles heavy on our souls. It is in those low places that faith is tested, refined, and often made more real than it ever was on the mountaintop.

Grief ushers us into the valley in ways we never expect. Loss shakes the ground beneath us, causing us to question not only our future but sometimes even our God. We wonder where He is when the tears won't stop. We whisper prayers that seem to fall into silence. We long for His nearness and wonder why He feels so far away. In those moments, faith can feel fragile—like a flickering flame fighting against the wind.

Yet the valley is also the place where God draws close. Psalm 23 reminds us, *"Even though I walk through the valley of the shadow of death, I will fear no evil, for you are with me."* Notice that David does not say he avoided the valley or escaped it quickly. He walked through it, and it was in that walking that he discovered God's presence most intimately. The valley, as painful as it is, becomes the very place where God's promises prove true.

Faith in the valley rarely looks bold or triumphant. More often, it looks like surrender—a quiet trust that even here, even now, God is still good.

When my heart was broken in loss, I learned that faith in the valley isn't about having all the answers. It isn't about feeling strong or certain. It's about choosing—one fragile step at a time—to lean on the God who promises never to leave us. Some days that choice looked like whispering a single prayer: *"Lord, help me breathe today."* Other days it was simply opening my Bible and clinging to a verse that reminded me of His love. Faith in the valley rarely looks bold or triumphant. More often, it looks like surrender—a quiet trust that even here, even now, God is still good.

Valley faith is a stripped-down faith. It teaches us that God is not only the God of miracles and mountaintops but also the God who sits with us in sorrow. Jesus Himself was called *"a man of sorrows, acquainted with grief"* (Isaiah 53:3). He knows the valley firsthand. He doesn't stand at a distance calling us to climb out of our despair—He walks with us through it, bearing the weight of our pain.

There is something profoundly comforting in knowing that God understands grief. When Jesus wept at the tomb of Lazarus (John 11:35), He showed us that tears are not weakness—they are love poured out. In the valley, our tears become prayers, and our cries become offerings that the Shepherd gathers tenderly.

The valley can even become holy ground. It is the place where we discover that God's strength is made perfect in our weakness. It's where His presence becomes more precious than answers, and where we begin to trust Him not because life is easy, but because He is faithful. Paul reminds us of this paradox when he writes, *"For when I am weak, then I am strong"* (2 Corinthians 12:10). In the valley, this truth comes alive—we learn that God's power is not diminished by our sorrow but revealed through it.

Faith in the valley doesn't mean we stop grieving. It doesn't silence our cries or erase the ache. It means we believe that even in our grief, God is holding us close. It's the assurance that our tears don't fall unseen, that our prayers do not drift unheard, and that our Shepherd will guide us—step by step—until light breaks through the shadows again.

When I look back now, I can see how the valley, though painful and dark, was also a sacred classroom. It was there that I learned dependence, surrender, and a deeper kind of faith—the kind that clings when everything else has fallen away. The valley may not feel holy while you're walking through it, but one day, as you glance back over your shoulder, you'll see the faint glimmer of grace woven through every step.

The same God who meets us on the mountain is the One who kneels beside us in the valley. He doesn't waste our tears. He redeems them, using even our deepest pain to draw us closer to His heart. And in time, when we emerge from the shadows into the light, we realize we were never alone. The Shepherd was there all along—guiding, comforting, and carrying us until faith once again became sight.

CLOSING REFLECTION

The valleys of grief are some of the hardest places we will ever walk, but they are not without meaning. In those deep shadows, faith becomes real, raw, and resilient. It is not the polished faith of mountaintops but the steady, trembling faith of those who know their Shepherd is nearby. Take heart: your valley is not forever, and you do not walk it alone.

"The Lord is my light and my salvation—whom shall I fear? The Lord is the stronghold of my life—of whom shall I be afraid?" (Psalm 27:1)

Father, you are the God of the valleys as well as the mountaintops. When my faith feels fragile and my heart is heavy, remind me that you are near. Teach me to trust you even when I cannot see the way forward. Strengthen my faith to believe that your presence is enough and that your love will carry me through. May my valley become a place where I encounter you more deeply, and may I walk through it with the assurance that you will never let me go.

Amen.

CHAPTER THIRTY-SIX

The God Who Draws Near

SUFFERING HAS A WAY OF making us feel abandoned. The silence after prayers, the emptiness of an unfilled chair, the hollow echo of a house without the one we love—all these moments can whisper the lie that God has left us. Grief is not just the absence of someone dear, it can feel like the absence of God Himself.

As I've continued through the grief journey, the words from Psalm 34:18 have become my constant go-to. Those words are a promise God has given us, and one that I have often reminded Him of. They have carried me in the darkest nights of grief. Even when I couldn't sense His presence, I had to trust that He was there. Sometimes God's nearness is not felt in the dramatic or the miraculous, but in the quiet, sustaining ways He holds us together when everything in us feels like it's falling apart.

I remember nights when the tears would not stop, when loneliness wrapped itself around me like a heavy blanket. In those moments, I didn't always hear God's voice or feel His hand in some tangible way, but somehow, I made it through the night. Somehow, I found the strength to face the next day. That, too, was His nearness. His presence was not absent—it was simply expressed in the strength He gave me to endure what I thought I could not.

The God who draws near often reveals Himself through people as well. A friend who calls at just the right moment. A meal that shows up on the doorstep. A handwritten card that arrives on a day when the sorrow feels especially sharp or the sweet unexpected invitation to join a friend for a cup of tea. These are not flukes—they are reminders that God sees us and chooses to show His love through the hands and voices of others. His nearness is not always in the thunder or the fire; more often it is in the gentle whisper, like Elijah heard on the mountain (1 Kings 19:11–12).

When we are crushed in spirit, we long for God to take away the pain. And while He doesn't always remove suffering, He promises His presence within it. This is what makes His nearness so profound. He is not a distant God observing from afar but Emmanuel, God with us. Jesus Himself entered into our suffering. He wept at the tomb of His friend. He carried the cross. He bore the weight of sorrow and sin so that we would never have to walk through our valleys alone.

In suffering, the God who draws near becomes our lifeline. We may not always recognize His presence in the moment, but when we look back, we often see that He was holding us all along. Every breath we took when grief felt suffocating, every moment of comfort that broke through the darkness, every reminder of hope—these were His fingerprints, evidence of a love that refuses to leave us.

To know that God draws near is to know that we are never truly abandoned. His presence is not dependent on how strong our faith feels in the moment, nor is it diminished by our questions or doubts. Even when we are too weak to pray, too weary to lift our heads, He leans in close, whispering His love over us. The truth is, His nearness is less about our ability to feel Him and more about His faithfulness to never let us go.

The truth is, His nearness is less about
our ability to feel Him and more about His
faithfulness to never let us go.

If you are walking through suffering today, know this: God is nearer than you think. He is not only beside you, He is within you, sustaining you, comforting you, and carrying you when you cannot carry yourself. His nearness is the steady truth that suffering cannot erase.

CLOSING REFLECTION

Grief may tell us we are abandoned, but God promises we are never alone. He draws near in ways both quiet and profound—in the strength that gets us through another day, in the kindness of a friend, in the peace that comes when we least expect it. He is Emmanuel, the God who is with us in every valley. Take courage in His promise:

"Never will I leave you; never will I forsake you" (Hebrews 13:5).

PRAYER FOR THE JOURNEY

Lord, thank you for drawing near to the brokenhearted
and for holding close those who are crushed in spirit.
When I cannot feel your presence, remind me of your
promises. Teach me to trust that you are with me even in
the silence and sorrow. Let me recognize your nearness in
the gentle ways you provide strength, comfort, and peace.
May my suffering become a place where I encounter your
love more deeply, and may I rest in the assurance that I
am never alone. Amen.

CHAPTER THIRTY-SEVEN

Holding Fast in the Storm

WHEN THE STORMS OF GRIEF roll in, they can feel relentless, pounding against the walls of your heart until you wonder if you'll have the strength to stand. The sky darkens, the wind howls, and the waves rise higher than you think you can endure. It's in these moments we feel small and powerless against a force so much bigger than ourselves.

But every sailor knows that survival in the storm depends on one thing—the anchor. Without it, you're tossed aimlessly, drifting farther from shore. With it, you may still be battered by the waves, but you remain grounded, tethered to something solid beneath the surface.

For those of us navigating grief, Jesus becomes that anchor. Hebrews 6:19 calls Him *"an anchor for the soul, firm and secure."* He doesn't still every storm the moment it appears, but He holds us steady through it. His promises keep us from being swept away by fear, regret, or hopelessness.

Anchoring in Him doesn't mean we won't feel the sting of the wind or the crash of the waves. It means that, no matter how fierce the storm, we are held. Even when we can't see the shoreline, we can trust that His hands will not let us go.

> But when we anchor to Christ, we find a
> security that no wave can undo. His love,
> His Word, His presence becomes the rock
> beneath the waters.

I can remember seasons when the waves of sorrow felt endless, when one day blurred into another, and the ache seemed impossible to carry. In those moments, I found that "holding fast" didn't mean I had to feel strong. Sometimes it was simply whispering His name when I had no other words. Other times, it meant clinging to one verse of Scripture that felt like a lifeline and repeating it until peace began to steady me. Often, it was leaning on the prayers of friends when my own faith felt faint.

The storms of grief are not only emotional, they are spiritual. They test our foundations and ask us what, or who, we are truly tethered to. If we anchor ourselves to temporary things—our own strength, the approval of others, or even the hope that life will go back to normal, the storms will inevitably pull us away. But when we anchor to Christ, we find a security that no wave can undo. His love, His Word, His presence becomes the rock beneath the waters.

What's remarkable about anchors is that their work is unseen. Buried beneath the surface, out of sight, they quietly keep the vessel from drifting away. In the same way, the anchor of Christ's love may not always feel visible in our darkest storms, but it is always holding us steady. Even when we cannot see how, He is keeping us from being swept into desolation.

Storms can feel long, and they often come without warning. Some are sudden, crashing into our lives without preparation. Others are slow and lingering, stretching on for months or even years. But Scripture assures us that none of them are greater than the power of Christ. In Mark 4:39, Jesus stood in the boat with His disciples, rebuked the wind, and stilled the sea with a word: *"Quiet! Be still!"* That same voice speaks over our storms today.

The storms will come and some will feel longer than we can

bear, but we don't face them alone. With our anchor set deep in the unshakable love of God, we can weather the waves and wait for the dawn. The sky will not always be dark. The storm will not always rage. And until it passes, Christ will hold us fast.

CLOSING REFLECTION

Grief's storms are fierce, but they are never final. In the hands of Jesus, our anchor, we are steady even when the winds howl and the waves rise high. We are not defined by the storm, but by the One who holds us secure within it. Take heart in this promise:

"When you pass through the waters, I will be with you; and when you pass through the rivers, they will not sweep over you" (Isaiah 43:2).

PRAYER FOR THE JOURNEY

Lord, when the waves of grief rise high and the winds
threaten to carry me away, be my anchor. Hold me steady
in your truth when I feel lost and adrift. Remind me
that no storm is stronger than your love. Keep my heart
tethered to you until the skies clear and the waters still.
Amen.

CHAPTER THIRTY-EIGHT

Anchored in Peace

I KNOW I'VE OFTEN MENTIONED that grief feels like being tossed in a storm. That's because it has always seemed to be one of the best analogies as I've walked this grief journey. The winds of sorrow batter us, the waves of despair threaten to pull us under, and stability seems impossible to find. Yet in the midst of the storm, Scripture reminds us that Christ is our strong tower, our safe refuge, the One who anchors us in peace. Proverbs 18:10 declares, *"The name of the Lord is a fortified tower; the righteous run to it and are safe."*

When we're in the midst of a storm, with Jesus by our side, His peace finds a way to calm us. Yet, peace in grief does not mean the absence of tears. It does not mean the ache disappears or that the questions suddenly fade. Instead, peace is the calm assurance that even in sorrow, we are held.

Still, there were nights when my heart felt like it would break under the weight of loss, no words that could soothe me, and no distraction that could ease the pain. But in prayer—sometimes only a whispered, "Jesus, help me"—I felt His peace settle over me like the warmest blanket. It didn't erase the grief, but it reminded me that He was right there beside me. His presence became the tower I could run to, the anchor that held me firm.

Paul describes this supernatural peace in Philippians 4:7: *"And the peace of God, which transcends all understanding, will guard your hearts and your minds in Christ Jesus."* This peace does not come from circumstances improving—it comes from Christ Himself. It is unexplainable to the world, yet undeniable to those who experience it.

And as we lean into His presence, we find that peace is not fragile—it is strong and unshakable, able to hold us through the fiercest storms.

The day after Melanie ran ahead to Heaven, I experienced His peace in a way I had never felt before. Oh, I was very familiar with this scripture and had quoted it multiple times over the years. But, this peace—it was much more than words on the pages in the Bible. It was a living thing that is hard to describe even today. He covered me in a way that brought a calmness over me even though everything around me in the natural was upended. His peace brought a sense of warmth and security that confirmed He was not only beside me, but carrying me every step of the way. Only His peace was able to provide a comfort as He whispered that my girl was with Him, and everything was going to be alright.

Anchoring ourselves in peace requires a choice. We can choose to run to Him rather than trying to weather the storm on our own. And, we can choose to trust that His promises are true, even when feelings say otherwise. This doesn't mean the storm immediately stops raging—it means that while the winds rage, our souls remain tethered to something greater than the storm. And as we lean into His presence, we find that peace is not fragile—it is strong and unshakable, able to hold us through the fiercest storms.

I have also learned that His peace often comes in the small, quiet ways as I sit in His presence. It shows up in a verse that meets me right where I am. Music has always been an important part of my healing journey and it often comes in a song that seems written for my aching heart. It arrives in the kindness of a friend who doesn't try to fix me but simply sits with me. These are all whispers of His presence, steady reminders that He is near, and that His peace is still anchoring me even when the storm rages.

That peace also becomes a witness to others. When people see us walking through grief with a quiet steadiness, not because of our own strength but because of Christ, they are drawn to the Source of that peace. Our lives testify that the storms of life are real, but so is the God who holds us fast. And sometimes, our testimony of peace in the storm gives someone else the courage to cling to Him in their storm as well.

Grief will always bring waves, but peace reminds us that we don't have to be tossed endlessly by them. No matter how fierce the winds, the anchor holds. And one day, the storms will cease completely. Revelation 21:4 promises us that the day will come when *"He will wipe every tear from their eyes. There will be no more death or mourning or crying or pain."* Until then, we can rest in the assurance that Christ, our strong tower, will never fail us.

CLOSING REFLECTION

Lord, thank you for being my strong tower in the storms of grief. When the winds of sorrow rage and I feel unsteady, anchor me in your peace. Guard my heart with the assurance that you are near and will never let me go. Help me to trust your promises even when the waves rise high, and let my life reflect the strength of your presence. Keep me steady until the day when the storms are no more and I am safe in your eternal embrace.

"We have this hope as an anchor for the soul, firm and secure." (Hebrews 6:19)

PRAYER FOR THE JOURNEY

Lord, thank you for being my refuge and strong tower. When the storms of grief rise around me, anchor me in your peace. Guard my heart and mind with the assurance that I am safe in you. Help me to run to you daily, finding in your presence the calm my soul longs for. May my life reflect your unshakable peace to a world that desperately needs it. Amen.

PART EIGHT

Beauty, Growth, and Renewal

CHAPTER THIRTY-NINE

Beauty from Ashes

HEALING IS NEVER ABOUT RETURNING to who we once were before loss touched our lives. Grief changes us; it reshapes our hearts and alters our vision of the world. Yet in the midst of that reshaping, God does something astonishing. He takes what feels broken beyond repair and begins to weave it into something new, something we never could have imagined. Scripture captures this hope in Psalm 30:11: *"You turned my wailing into dancing; you removed my sackcloth and clothed me with joy."* What feels like only sorrow and ruin, God has the power to transform into something beautiful—joy born not from denial of pain, but from His redeeming presence in the midst of it.

Ashes are what remain after fire has consumed everything. They represent ruin, destruction, and the places in our lives where we feel stripped bare. When we grieve, it often feels like everything has been reduced to ashes—the plans we made, the future we dreamed, the sense of normal we once knew. Yet God, in His mercy, does not leave us in the ashes. He bends low, gathers what is left, and begins the miraculous work of turning even devastation into beauty.

For me, the ashes were the unbearable emptiness of my daughter's absence. I couldn't see beyond the pain; it felt as though the fire had consumed every joy I had ever known. And yet, as I moved forward, I began to notice glimmers of beauty breaking through. It was in the friendships that deepened because someone dared to walk beside me in grief. It was in the courage to speak Melanie's name, telling her story so that her life continued to impact others. It was in the hope that anchored me, reminding me that this separation is not forever. This is just a pause, until I see her again. Those glimmers did not erase the ashes, but they reminded me that God was still at work, planting beauty in the very soil of my sorrow.

This beauty is not shallow or fragile—it is the beauty of resilience, compassion, and testimony. Scars become stories, reminders of where we have been and of the God who carried us through. Each scar speaks: *Here is where I thought I was finished, but God was faithful. Here is where despair threatened to win, but God's grace was greater.* What once felt like wreckage becomes the very testimony that declares His power to redeem.

The transformation from ashes to beauty does not happen quickly. It is slow and often hidden, like seeds pushing through the soil. But as time unfolds, we begin to see the evidence: a softened heart toward others who are hurting, a deeper reliance on God, a willingness to share our journey so others may find hope. That is beauty from ashes.

Only God can take what was meant to destroy us and turn it into something that speaks of His glory. Only He can transform suffering into a story of hope. And when He does, our lives become living testimonies—not of our strength, but of His redeeming love.

The ashes remain part of our story. We don't ever forget. We do not erase the pain or pretend it never existed. But God takes those ashes, infuses them with His Spirit, and writes a greater ending. He doesn't discard our sorrow. He redeems it. And the beauty that emerges is more profound because it has been born out of fire.

The transformation from ashes to beauty does not happen quickly. It is slow and often hidden, like seeds pushing through the soil.

CLOSING REFLECTION

God's promise in Psalm 30 is not wishful thinking—it is a declaration of His heart for the broken. He longs to replace despair with joy, ruin with restoration, and ashes with beauty. If you are still standing in the ashes of loss, do not give up hope. Trust that the same God who raised beauty from the ruins of Calvary can bring renewal to your story as well. His glory is revealed not in the absence of suffering, but in His power to transform it.

"He has made everything beautiful in its time" (Ecclesiastes 3:11).

PRAYER FOR THE JOURNEY

Lord, thank you that you are the God who brings beauty from ashes. When all I see is devastation, remind me that you are still at work, redeeming my sorrow and writing a story of hope. Teach me to see the beauty you are planting in my broken places, and let my scars become testimonies of your faithfulness. May my life declare that no loss is beyond your power to restore. Amen.

CHAPTER FORTY

The Slow Work of Healing

HEALING IS A WORD THAT sounds hopeful, yet for the grieving heart, it can also feel out of reach. In the wake of deep loss, we long for relief, for the heaviness to lift, for our hearts to feel whole again. Healing does come, but not come quickly, nor does it come all at once. It is a slow work—sometimes so slow that we hardly notice it until we look back and realize that the rawness has softened, that the sharp edges of sorrow are not quite as jagged as before.

When I first began walking the grief journey, I often heard the phrase, *"Time heals all wounds."* But I now know that isn't true. Time alone does not heal. Time simply passes. True healing comes from the Lord, who gently tends to our brokenness with patience and love. He does not rush us through our sorrow or scold us for still feeling the ache months or even years later. Instead, He meets us where we are, carrying us step by step through the valley. Healing is His work in us, and it unfolds in His timing.

One of the greatest challenges of grief is accepting that healing will not erase the loss. The person we love is still gone, and no amount of time will change that reality. Healing does not mean forgetting; it means learning to live with the love and the loss woven together in our hearts. The tears may come less often, but the love remains just as strong. Healing teaches us that it is possible to live fully, even while carrying sorrow.

Healing does not mean forgetting; it means learning to live with the love and the loss woven together in our hearts.

God's Word reminds us of His tender care in this process. In Jeremiah 30:17, the Lord promises, *"But I will restore you to health and heal your wounds," declares the Lord*. Notice that it is God Himself who does the restoring and the healing. Like a physician who patiently tends a wound, He leans close, applying the balm of His presence, wrapping us in His promises, and allowing us space to mend. The scars may remain, but even scars can tell a story of survival and of God's faithfulness.

The slow work of healing is also seen in small, everyday moments that begin to feel lighter. The first time you laugh without guilt. The day you can look at a picture without breaking down completely. The ability to enjoy a gathering with friends without feeling consumed by absence. These moments don't erase the grief, but they reveal that healing is taking root. They are signs that God is gently stitching together what has been torn.

Healing also reshapes us. We don't return to who we were before the loss, nor should we try. Instead, healing transforms us into people who carry deeper compassion, stronger faith, and greater awareness of what truly matters. Grief changes us, but healing shows us that change can carry beauty. We become living testimonies of endurance, resilience, and grace, not because we escaped the valley, but because God walked us through it.

We often want healing to be quick and complete, but God knows that deep love requires deep healing. And deep healing takes time. The slowness of it is not a punishment—it is an act of mercy. For in the slow work, He draws us near, teaches us to depend on Him daily, and reveals Himself in ways we might never have known otherwise.

So, if you find yourself wondering why it still hurts, why healing feels so far away, take heart. God is not finished with you yet. He is working even now, slowly, patiently, tenderly, until the day when all sorrow will cease and every tear will be wiped away. Healing may take longer than you ever imagined, but it will come, because the One who promised is faithful.

CLOSING REFLECTION

Lord, thank you that you are the Healer of broken hearts and the Restorer of wounded souls. Teach me to trust the slow work of healing, even when it feels hidden and unfinished. Help me to notice the small signs of your presence, the gentle ways you are mending what grief has torn. Give me patience with myself as I wait for your timing, and remind me that your work in me is not yet complete. Anchor me in the hope of your promise:

"He who began a good work in you will carry it on to completion until the day of Christ Jesus" (Philippians 1:6)

PRAYER FOR THE JOURNEY

Heavenly Father, thank you for being patient with me in my grief. Teach me to trust your slow and steady work of healing, even when progress feels hard to see. Bind up the broken places in my heart with your love, and remind me that scars are not signs of failure but of survival. Help me to walk each day with hope, believing that you are mending me, little by little, until the day when sorrow is no more. Amen.

CHAPTER FORTY-ONE

Learning to Live Again

AFTER THE STORMS OF GRIEF begin to quiet, the silence can feel almost foreign. The days may not be as overwhelming, yet you find yourself standing in the middle of life's landscape, unsure if you're ready to take that next step forward. You've been in survival mode for so long, simply trying to make it through each day, that the thought of fully living again can feel both hopeful and frightening.

In grief, healing isn't a single moment where the pain disappears. It's a gradual, often hesitant process, learning to loosen the tight grip on sorrow just enough to let joy back in, and trusting that the One who carried you through the darkness can also lead you into light.

The first attempts at living again might be small. You might allow yourself to laugh without feeling guilty. You might say yes to meeting a friend for coffee. You might revisit a place that holds memories and find that you can breathe there. Perhaps you'll return to a hobby you once found great joy in. These steps, though simple, are monumental. They mark the quiet return of life into your heart.

There is often a strange mixture of emotions when life begins to feel lighter. Guilt may creep in, whispering that moving forward means leaving your loved one behind. But this is not true. Learning to live again is not forgetting. It's actually carrying their memory with you in new ways, allowing their influence and love to shape who you are becoming. Their presence remains etched into your story, woven into your words, your actions, and your everyday moments.

Living again may look like finding new purpose, new rhythms, or even new dreams. But all of these grow out of the deep soil of love and loss. They are not separate from your grief; they are born through it. What once felt impossible begins to look like resilience—proof that sorrow may shape you, but it does not have to silence you.

And here is the beautiful truth: we don't take these steps alone. The same God who was our shelter in the storm becomes our guide in the stillness. He does not just rescue us from the flood; He leads us into spacious places where our souls can breathe again. As Isaiah 58:11 promises, *"The Lord will guide you always; he will satisfy your needs in a sun-scorched land and will strengthen your frame. You will be like a well-watered garden, like a spring whose waters never fail."*

There will still be hard days. Grief has a way of returning when we least expect it, but each time it does, you'll remember the strength you've found before. Healing is not about forgetting the valley—it's about remembering who walked with you through it. When you question whether you can take another step, look in the rearview mirror and see how far you've come. You are not standing where you started. Every tear, every prayer, every moment of survival has brought you here. And with each new step, you'll grow a little stronger, trust a little deeper, and believe more fully that even in the ache, life is still worth living.

> What once felt impossible begins to look like resilience—proof that sorrow may shape you, but it does not have to silence you.

Learning to live again is not a betrayal of the past—it is an act of hope for the future. It is a declaration that love is stronger than death, that faith is stronger than despair, and that God's promises are strong enough to carry you into what lies ahead.

CLOSING REFLECTION

Moving from survival to living again is not a single step but a journey of trust. As God gently leads us forward, He helps us honor the love we carry while embracing the life that remains. In His timing, sorrow gives way to courage, and we begin to see that living fully is another way of loving deeply. His grace reminds us that healing does not mean forgetting—it means learning to live again with hope.

"The Lord will guide you always; he will satisfy your needs in a sun-scorched land." (Isaiah 58:11)

PRAYER FOR THE JOURNEY

Lord, you know the depth of my sorrow and the weight of my loss. Thank you for holding me through the hardest days and for patiently guiding me toward life again. Give me the courage to take each small step forward, trusting that you walk beside me. Let my days be filled with quiet moments of joy, and may my heart always carry the love of the one I miss so dearly. Amen.

CHAPTER FORTY-TWO

Rebuilding Who You Are

WHEN SOMEONE YOU LOVE DIES, a part of you changes forever. Life is split into two timelines: before and after. In the before, your identity was woven together with theirs—your roles, your routines, and even your dreams were connected. In the after, you may find yourself asking, *Who am I now? Am I still a mom, a wife, a sister, a partner?*

Death doesn't just take the person we love, it can feel like it takes parts of us as well. The way we once moved through the world no longer feels familiar. Things that once defined us might seem irrelevant, and places that once brought joy may now feel foreign. It's disorienting, even frightening, to realize you must rediscover who you are without them physically here.

Rebuilding your identity after loss takes time and doesn't happen overnight. It begins with small acts of self-compassion, allowing yourself to explore, to try, and sometimes to fail. You might rediscover hobbies you once loved but set aside long ago. You might take on new roles or responsibilities that stretch you in unexpected ways. You might simply start by asking, *What matters most to me today?*

This journey isn't about moving on or erasing the past. It's about integrating your loss into the fabric of your life in a way that honors your loved one while also allowing you to grow. They are still part of your story, but now your story is unfolding in a new chapter.

As you rebuild, you may notice that loss has changed your perspective. You might care less about things that once consumed your energy and more about what truly matters—relationships, purpose, and faith. God often uses grief to refine us, shaping us into people who live with deeper compassion, clearer priorities, and a greater awareness of eternity.

Rebuilding can feel fragile at first. There may be days when you feel strong and others when you collapse under the weight of absence. Both are part of the process. Each time you rise, even shakily, you prove to yourself that you can live in this "after." And slowly, a new version of you begins to emerge—one who is both broken and beautiful, marked by scars yet full of resilience.

Scripture reminds us that we are never left to rebuild alone. In Isaiah 58:12, God gives this promise: *"Your people will rebuild the ancient ruins and will raise up the age-old foundations; you will be called Repairer of Broken Walls, Restorer of Streets with Dwellings."* Though spoken to Israel, the truth extends to us as well—God is in the work of restoration. Where grief has torn down, He helps us rise again. Where loss has left ruins, He builds foundations for a future still filled with purpose.

This journey isn't about moving on or erasing the past. It's about integrating your loss into the fabric of your life in a way that honors your loved one while also allowing you to grow.

You are still you, but you are also becoming someone new, someone shaped by love, strengthened by sorrow, and guided by God's hand into the life that still awaits you. Rebuilding is not about losing who you were but discovering who you are becoming in the wake of both love and loss.

And while the rebuilding is slow, it is also sacred. Every step forward honors both your loved one's memory and God's promise that life, even after death, still holds meaning.

CLOSING REFLECTION

Lord, thank you that even in the ruins of grief, you are at work rebuilding my heart and shaping my life. When I feel lost in this "after," remind me that my identity is secure in you. Teach me to embrace both the love I carry from the past and the life you are guiding me into now. Help me walk forward with courage, knowing that even in sorrow, you are making me new.

"Do not fear, for I have redeemed you; I have summoned you by name; you are mine." (Isaiah 43:1)

PRAYER FOR THE JOURNEY

Lord, I confess that sometimes I don't recognize myself anymore. The loss I've endured has changed me in ways I'm still trying to understand. Help me to trust that you are rebuilding my life and my identity in your perfect timing. Give me courage to embrace the person I'm becoming, and may my life honor both you and the memory of the one I love. Amen.

CHAPTER FORTY-THREE

Finding Purpose in the After

WHEN GRIEF IS FRESH, THE very idea of purpose can feel almost offensive. In the early days, you're simply trying to survive, not searching for meaning. Just getting out of bed or making it through the day feels monumental. To talk about purpose in the middle of such pain can feel like a burden you're not ready to carry.

But as time gently moves forward, as the rawness begins to soften, you may notice a stirring, an invitation to live not just through the pain, but beyond it. This stirring isn't about rushing your healing or minimizing your loss. It is about discovering that, even in the wake of heartbreak, God isn't done with you yet. He is still writing a story with your life.

Finding purpose after loss is not about replacing what was lost or forcing yourself into a new mission. Nothing and no one can ever take the place of the person you love. Purpose in the after is about listening for the quiet ways God might be calling you to use what you've been through—the lessons learned, the compassion that has grown deeper, the understanding of pain you now carry, to make a difference in ways both big and small.

Sometimes, purpose looks like sharing your story so someone else feels less alone. Your vulnerability becomes a lifeline for someone drowning in sorrow. Sometimes, it's creating something beautiful out of what was broken—a ministry, a book, a painting, a tradition that keeps their memory alive. And sometimes, purpose is found in the simple, quiet ways you show up differently in the world—loving people more fiercely, cherishing small moments, and living with greater intentionality because you know how fragile life really is.

Purpose in the after is about listening for the quiet ways God might be calling you to use what you've been through.

Your purpose may not arrive as a grand vision or a neatly outlined plan. More often, it comes as a small nudge. A conversation you can't shake. An opportunity that stirs your heart. A cause that suddenly matters to you in a new way. These are the seeds God plants in the soil of your sorrow, and gradually they can grow into something meaningful that gives your days new direction.

It's important to remember that purpose is not static. It evolves as you do. What matters most in one season may shift in the next. In one chapter, your purpose may be to rest, to heal, and to simply keep going. In another, it may expand into reaching out, creating, serving, or building something that blesses others. Through it all, your loved one's influence continues to shape the way you live, love, and serve. Their story is woven into yours, and the way you live out your purpose carries their legacy forward.

Grief changes us, but it can also awaken us. This awakening took me by surprise as it strips away what is unimportant and sharpens our focus on what truly matters. I no longer sweat the small stuff and my perspective on what is truly important in life has changed exponentially. Purpose in the after is not about erasing the ache. It is about allowing the ache to deepen the way you live, to tenderize your heart toward others, and to remind you of the eternal perspective that love and life are gifts not to be taken for granted.

God's word assures us that nothing is wasted in His hands. Romans 8:28 reminds us: *"And we know that in all things God works for the good of those who love him, who have been called according to his purpose."* This doesn't mean everything that happens is good. Loss will never feel good. But it does mean that God can weave even the darkest valleys into something that reflects His glory and brings hope to others.

Finding purpose in the after is about trusting that God can bring light out of even the deepest darkness. It is choosing to believe that your story is not over, that your days still hold meaning, and that the love you carry is meant to ripple outward.

CLOSING REFLECTION

Finding purpose after loss is not something we chase; it's something God unfolds as we begin to heal. In the quiet spaces of grief, He plants seeds that will one day grow into meaning we could never have imagined. As we trust Him with our pain, He reshapes our hearts for compassion, deepens our capacity to love, and reminds us that life still holds beauty and calling. Even in the after, God is writing a new story — one marked by grace, courage, and hope.

"The Lord will fulfill his purpose for me; your steadfast love, O Lord, endures forever." Psalm 138:8

PRAYER FOR THE JOURNEY

Lord, thank you for the promise that my life still has meaning, even after loss. I don't always know where you are leading me, but I trust that you can use my pain for a greater good. Help me to listen for your voice, to follow where you guide, and to live each day in a way that honors both you and the one I miss so deeply. Amen.

CHAPTER FORTY-FOUR

Turning Pain into Purpose

PAIN WAS NEVER PART OF God's original design for our lives. He created us for wholeness, for joy, and for unbroken fellowship with Him and with one another. But in this broken world, sorrow inevitably finds us. Loss carves its way into our stories, leaving us with wounds that change us forever. And yet, the miracle of God's grace is that He doesn't waste a single tear. In His hands, even our deepest pain can be transformed into purpose.

When my daughter died, I couldn't see beyond the devastation. Every day felt like survival, and the thought of finding purpose in such loss almost felt disrespectful. How could anything good ever come from something so crushing? The emptiness was overwhelming, and hope seemed far away. But then, as God began to gently bind up the raw edges of my grief, I realized that my story, the very thing I once wished I could escape, was the very tool God wanted to use. My pain became the platform through which I could reach others who were hurting. What I thought would always be my greatest weakness became the place where God's strength shone the brightest.

This is the mysterious way God works. He takes what was meant for harm and turns it into something that bears fruit. Joseph said it best when he looked back on years of betrayal and suffering: *"You intended to harm me, but God intended it for good to accomplish what is now being done, the saving of many lives"* (Genesis 50:20). What was once only pain became the seed of purpose.

Turning pain into purpose doesn't mean we are glad for our suffering. It doesn't mean we stop missing the one we've lost or that the ache goes away. What it means is that our story is not wasted. Our tears can water seeds of comfort in someone else's life. Our scars become signposts pointing others to hope. Our testimonies declare that God is able to redeem even the darkest valleys.

Purpose may come in small ways. It may look like sitting beside another person who is grieving and letting them weep, knowing you don't need to fix their pain because you've been there too. It may be writing a card, sharing a memory, leading a support group, or simply being brave enough to say, *"I understand."* Each act, no matter how small, becomes part of the redemptive work of God, using what once broke us to now bless others.

In time, our pain-turned-purpose also becomes worship. It is our way of saying, *"Lord, I do not understand why this happened, but I trust you enough to place even this into your hands. Use it as you will."* There is no greater testimony of faith than allowing God to redeem what the enemy meant for destruction and to let His light shine through our broken places.

I have seen God bring beauty out of ashes through the most unexpected moments—through conversations that gave someone courage to keep going, through words I wrote that touched a heart across the world, through opportunities to come alongside others who thought they were alone in their grief. Each of these moments reminded me that while I never would have chosen this road, God is still able to bring meaning out of sorrow.

Our pain may remain part of us, but in God's hands, it is not the end of the story. Purpose grows out of sorrow, hope rises from despair, and what once felt like ashes becomes a platform for His glory. The transformation doesn't happen overnight, but slowly, steadily, His Spirit works within us, reshaping our grief into compassion, our wounds into wisdom, and our sorrow into service.

> Purpose grows out of sorrow, hope rises
> from despair, and what once felt like ashes
> becomes a platform for His glory.

This is the redemptive power of God: He turns mourning into ministry, brokenness into blessing, and pain into purpose. And in doing so, He reminds us that death does not have the final word—Jesus does.

CLOSING REFLECTION

God never wastes our pain. Even the deepest wounds can become places where His light shines through. As we surrender our sorrow to Him, He transforms our brokenness into blessing and our struggles into strength. Every scar becomes a quiet declaration of His faithfulness—proof that His love always has the final word.

"And we know that in all things God works for the good of those who love him." (Romans 8:28)

PRAYER FOR THE JOURNEY

Lord, I bring you my pain and lay it in your hands. I confess that I do not always understand how you could use something so heavy, but I choose to trust that you can redeem even this. Turn my sorrow into compassion, my wounds into testimony, and my scars into stories of hope for others. Use my life, Lord, not in spite of my pain but through it, for your glory. Amen.

CHAPTER FORTY-FIVE

A Testimony of Hope

EVERY STORY WE LIVE BECOMES part of the larger story God is writing. For those who walk through grief, that story often feels filled with pages of sorrow, questions, and silence. And yet, when we look back, we can see that even in the hardest chapters, God's hand has never left the page. It is from this truth that our lives become a testimony, not of perfection, not of strength, but of hope.

Hope, by definition, is forward-looking. It points us beyond our current sorrow to something more, something promised but not yet fully seen. As Paul writes in Romans 8:24, *"For in this hope we were saved. But hope that is seen is no hope at all. Who hopes for what they already have?"* Our testimony of hope is rooted not in what we can see today but in the assurance of God's promises—that there will be reunion, redemption, and eternal life in His presence.

There was a time when I couldn't imagine that one day my story would become a testimony that could encourage others. I only saw the pain, the emptiness, the ache that never seemed to ease. The idea that God could use my shattered heart and story to touch someone else felt unthinkable. But as time went on, and as God faithfully carried me, I realized that my survival itself was a testimony. Each day I kept breathing, each step I took forward, each prayer whispered in the dark became evidence that God was holding me.

And as I began to share my story, I discovered something beautiful: others found hope in my journey. My scars became not just reminders of loss but signposts pointing to God's faithfulness. The very cracks in my heart became the places where His light shone through most brightly. What I once thought would always represent only sorrow began to carry with it a quiet strength, a witness to the truth that God not only doesn't abandon His children, but carries them through the valley of the shadow of death.

When we allow our stories to be seen,
they become lanterns that light the way
for others still walking in darkness. This is
what it means to live as witnesses of hope.

A testimony of hope does not require eloquence or a platform. It begins simply with honesty—telling the truth about our grief and about the God who meets us in it. Sometimes it's as small as sitting across from another hurting soul and saying, *"I understand. I've been there too."* Sometimes it's sharing a verse that carried you when you couldn't carry yourself, or a worship song that lifted you up when you were feeling down. Sometimes it's just the quiet resilience of living each day with faith, letting others see that while grief remains, so does hope.

What makes our testimony powerful is not that we have all the answers, but that we cling to God in the midst of questions. Our hope does not deny our pain—it shines through it. When we allow our stories to be seen, they become lanterns that light the way for others still walking in darkness.

This is what it means to live as witnesses of hope. Your life, with all its losses and scars, is not a story of hopelessness but of God's sustaining grace. Every tear you've cried, every prayer you've prayed, every moment you've chosen to keep trusting, these are threads of hope woven into your testimony. And as you share them, you bear witness to a God who is faithful, a Savior who redeems, and a future where sorrow will be no more.

You may not feel strong, but strength is not the requirement. Availability is. God takes our willingness to share even the broken pieces of our story and uses them to encourage someone else who is wondering if they can survive. And in that moment, our pain is not wasted—it becomes purpose. Our grief is not meaningless—it becomes ministry.

In the end, our testimony of hope is really a testimony of Christ. It is His presence that carried us, His promises that sustained us, and His love that will one day turn every tear into joy. To tell our story becomes part of His story—a story that assures us that sorrow is not the end, for in Christ, life and love endure.

CLOSING REFLECTION

Every story redeemed by God becomes a testimony of His faithfulness. Though grief may have once written the heaviest chapters of our lives, hope now writes new ones—chapters that declare, **"God is not finished with me yet."** Our testimony of hope does not erase the pain we've known, but it transforms it. It tells the world that even in our brokenness, God's love endures, His promises stand, and His light still shines through.

"Those who sow with tears will reap with songs of joy." (*Psalm 126:5*)

PRAYER FOR THE JOURNEY

*Lord, thank you that my story, even with all its broken-
ness, can be used to declare your faithfulness. Help me
to see my life as a testimony of hope, not because I am
strong, but because you are. Give me courage to share
my scars, my struggles, and my healing, so that others
may see your light shining through me. May my life point
always to you, the source of true and everlasting hope.*
Amen.

PART NINE

Living with Eternal Perspective

CHAPTER FORTY-SIX

Living with Eternal Perspective

GRIEF HAS A WAY OF narrowing our vision. When sorrow is fresh, all we can see is the empty chair, the silence where laughter once rang, the aching absence that fills every room. The days feel long, and the nights even longer. It can feel impossible to imagine a future that holds anything but pain. Yet as followers of Christ, we are invited to lift our eyes beyond the brokenness of this world and to live with an eternal perspective in mind.

An eternal perspective does not erase grief, it reframes it. It reminds us that this life is not the whole story, that what we endure here is temporary compared to the glory that awaits us. Paul wrote these words of encouragement to the Corinthians: *"For our light and momentary troubles are achieving for us an eternal glory that far outweighs them all. So, we fix our eyes not on what is seen, but on what is unseen, since what is seen is temporary, but what is unseen is eternal"* (2 Corinthians 4:17–18). To the grieving heart, troubles hardly feel "light and momentary," yet Paul's words remind us that compared to eternity with Christ, even our deepest sorrow is not the final word.

When my Melanie passed away, Heaven and eternity became more than just a theological concept—it became real in a way I had never felt before. I had always believed in Heaven, but in the shadow of loss, that promise took on a new depth. It meant that death was not the end. It meant that one day, I will see her again. That perspective did not take away my tears, but it gave me something to cling to, a lifeline for when despair threatened to drown me. It gave me hope that the separation is temporary and that reunion is certain in Christ. I began to view her absence as simply a pause in our time together, as I hold on to the God's promises, knowing I will be reunited with her again one day.

> An eternal perspective also allows us to carry our grief with hope. It doesn't minimize the pain of separation, but it reminds us that separation is not forever.

Living with eternity in view changes how we walk through each day. It softens our grip on the things of this world that once felt so important. Success, possessions, even the approval of others fade in comparison to the eternal reality that lies ahead. Instead, we begin to value what matters most: love, faith, and the legacy of Christ's presence in our lives. Our choices, our words, and our relationships take on eternal significance, because we recognize that this life is but a breath, preparing us for what is to come.

An eternal perspective also allows us to carry our grief with hope. It doesn't minimize the pain of separation, but it reminds us that separation is not forever. That promise of Revelation 21:4 assures us that every tear we cry now is noticed by God and will one day be wiped away by His own hand.

Even now, eternity reaches into the present. Each time we extend compassion, each time we choose forgiveness, each time we cling to hope, we are living as people of eternity. Our scars remind us of the brokenness of this world, but they also become testimonies of a greater story still unfolding—the story of God's redemption. And one day, every scar, every ache, every moment of longing will give way to wholeness in His presence.

For those who grieve, this perspective is not easy to hold. There will be days when the weight of loss presses hard and eternity feels far away. On those days, it is enough to whisper the promises of God back to ourselves: *"This is not forever. This is not the end. Jesus has conquered death."* Slowly, our gaze lifts from the emptiness of today to the fullness of eternity, and hope begins to rise again.

Grief may remind us of what has been taken, but faith reminds us of what still awaits. And as we keep our eyes fixed on Jesus, the One who has already gone ahead to prepare a place for us, we discover the courage to keep walking. This world is not our final home. Eternity with Him is.

CLOSING REFLECTION

Living with an eternal perspective does not take away our grief, but it gives us the lens through which to see beyond it. Death does not write the end of our story—Jesus does. He is the Alpha and the Omega, the beginning and the end, and His promise is sure: "And if I go and prepare a place for you, I will come back and take you to be with me that you also may be where I am" (John 14:3). With that assurance, we can carry both our sorrow and our hope, trusting that the best is yet to come.

"Do not be afraid. I am the First and the Last. I am the Living One; I was dead, and now look, I am alive forever and ever!" (Revelation 1:17-18)

PRAYER FOR THE JOURNEY

Father, help me to fix my eyes not on what is seen, but on what is unseen. When my heart aches with the weight of grief, remind me that eternity with you is my true home. Teach me to live each day with Heaven in mind, valuing what lasts forever and releasing what is temporary. Thank you for the promise of reunion, restoration, and joy in your presence. Until that day, strengthen me to live faithfully, carrying both grief and hope with my eyes lifted to eternity. Amen.

CHAPTER FORTY-SEVEN

Shining Light in the Darkness

WE CAN ALL ATTEST TO the fact that when loss enters your world, grief can feel like your world has gone completely dark. It feels like a heaviness that clouds the heart, a fog that obscures the path ahead. In those moments, hope seems distant, and joy feels like a memory. Yet into that darkness, Christ calls us to shine. Not because we are strong enough to produce our own light, but because His light dwells within us. Jesus said, *"You are the light of the world. A town built on a hill cannot be hidden"* (Matthew 5:14). Even in seasons of sorrow, His presence enables us to reflect a light that the darkness cannot overcome.

In my own grief, there were days when I wondered if my light had gone out completely. The pain was so heavy, the nights so long, that I felt empty and spent. But eventually, I came to understand that shining light in the darkness doesn't mean hiding behind a mask, forcing a smile, or pretending all is well. It means letting God's light shine through the cracks of my brokenness. It means being honest about the weight of the struggle, yet choosing to hold on to hope. Light in the darkness is not the denial of grief—it is the very presence of Christ within it.

This kind of light is powerful because it is authentic. People don't need to see a perfect faith—they need to see a persevering faith. They need to see that it is possible to walk through valleys and still trust God, to feel sorrow and still cling to hope. Our willingness to live openly with both grief and faith becomes a lantern for others, showing them that darkness is not the end of the story.

Sometimes shining light looks like sharing our story, letting others know that they are not alone in their pain. Sometimes it looks like offering kindness even when our own hearts are still tender. Sometimes it is as simple as choosing to rise each morning and walk forward with faith, even if our steps are slow. Every act of courage, every whispered prayer, every moment of trust becomes a flicker of light that pierces the night.

Light shines brightest where it is darkest. In our suffering, we carry a unique testimony of God's sustaining grace. Paul wrote, *"For God, who said, 'Let light shine out of darkness,' made his light shine in our hearts to give us the light of the knowledge of God's glory"* (2 Corinthians 4:6). Even when we feel fragile and weak, His light shines through us, often in ways we may not even realize.

I've come to see that shining light in the darkness is not about denying sorrow but about declaring that sorrow will not have the final word. The world is watching, not for perfect people, but for people who cling to hope in the face of life's challenges. Our brokenness becomes a canvas where God paints His glory, where His light shines all the more clearly because of our cracks.

When we allow His light to shine through our brokenness, others are drawn to the source of that light. They see not our strength, but His. And in this way, our grief becomes not just a private journey, but a testimony that points to the One who is faithful—the One who promises that darkness will never have the final word.

People don't need to see a perfect faith—
they need to see a persevering faith. They
need to see that it is possible to walk
through valleys and still trust God, to feel
sorrow and still cling to hope.

To shine light in the darkness is not to deny our sorrow—it is to proclaim that Jesus is greater than our sorrow. It is to trust that the same God who brings beauty from ashes can also turn our pain into a beacon of hope for others. And as we carry that light, we remind the world that Jesus is the true Light, and in Him, the darkness cannot win.

CLOSING REFLECTION

Even when grief surrounds us with shadows, God's light continues to shine. Through our weakness, His strength is revealed. Through our sorrow, His presence brings hope. As John's Gospel reminds us: **"The light shines in the darkness, and the darkness has not overcome it"** (John 1:5). May we carry that truth in our hearts, letting His light shine through us, even in the darkest night, so that others may see and be reminded that hope is never lost.

"You, Lord, keep my lamp burning; my God turns my darkness into light." (Psalm 18:28)

PRAYER FOR THE JOURNEY

Lord, thank you that your light shines even in the darkest valleys. When my own strength feels gone, let your light shine through me. Use my story, my scars, and even my weakness to reflect your hope to others. Teach me to live with courage, not hiding my grief, but allowing it to become a vessel of your love. May my life be a candle in the night, pointing always to you, the light of the world.

Amen.

CHAPTER FORTY-EIGHT

The Legacy of Love

EACH ACT OF REMEMBRANCE, EACH ritual of love, becomes part of a greater story—a legacy that outlives the years and carries forward into the lives we touch. Honoring our loved ones is not only about looking back, but also about how we choose to live today. The way we love, the way we serve, and the way we hold their memory shapes the legacy we continue to build. And in that legacy, their light still shines.

Love does not end with death. Though we grieve the absence of our loved ones, the love we shared with them continues to shape us, to ripple outward, and to leave an imprint on the world. This enduring impact is what we call legacy. It is not measured in wealth or possessions, but in the way love lives on through us.

When someone we cherish is gone, we often find ourselves reflecting on the lessons they left behind: the values they lived by, the kindness they offered, the faith they embodied. Their lives become a reminder that the most lasting legacy is not what we own, but how we love. Paul wrote in 1 Corinthians 13:13, *"And now these three remain: faith, hope and love. But the greatest of these is love."* Love is the thread that never breaks, the mark that endures through every season of life and beyond.

After my daughter's passing, I found myself clinging to the ways her life continues to speak. Though her time here was far too short, her joy, laughter, and tenderness left an indelible mark on everyone who knew her. The legacy of her love did not vanish when she left this earth. It continues through the stories we tell, the compassion we show, and the hope we hold onto. In that way, her life remains present, shaping mine in ways that keep me anchored in what matters most.

We are participants in a legacy that will outlast us, one that testifies to the faithfulness of God and the endurance of love.

The legacy of love also becomes our calling. As we grieve, we carry the responsibility of honoring the ones we've lost by living out the values they taught us. If they loved generously, we too can love generously. If they lived with courage, we can find ways to walk bravely. If they held onto faith, we can allow that faith to strengthen our own. In this way, their love multiplies, passed on from heart to heart, life to life.

God Himself designed love to be eternal. Romans 8:38–39 assures us that nothing—not death, nor life, nor anything else in all creation—can separate us from His love. That same divine love is what binds us to one another, even beyond the grave. The legacy of love is not simply memory; it is part of the eternal story God is weaving, one that will find its fulfillment when we are reunited in His presence.

Living in light of this truth transforms the way we walk through grief. The love we received and the love we continue to give are threads woven into something far greater than ourselves. We are participants in a legacy that will outlast us, one that testifies to the faithfulness of God and the endurance of love.

Every choice we make to forgive instead of resent, to encourage instead of despair, to give instead of withhold, becomes part of that legacy. In doing so, we ensure that the love we have received does not end with us but continues to bless others. And as we walk forward, we discover that we are not only remembering our loved ones—we are carrying their legacy into the future, letting it shine through our lives as a testimony of God's goodness and grace.

CLOSING REFLECTION

The greatest legacy we can leave or carry forward is love. It outlasts possessions, achievements, and even time itself. May we choose to honor our loved ones by living lives marked by compassion, courage, and faith, allowing their light to shine through us. And may we rest in the assurance that nothing, not even death, can separate us from the love of Christ, which binds us together forever.

"And over all these virtues put on love, which binds them all together in perfect unity." (Colossians 3:14)

PRAYER FOR THE JOURNEY

Lord, thank you for the gift of love that never ends. Help me honor the legacy of those I have lost by living in a way that reflects their love and, most of all, your love. Teach me to carry forward what they left behind—faith, courage, kindness, and compassion. May my life be a continuation of the love that has shaped me, leaving a testimony that points others to you. Amen.

CHAPTER FORTY-NINE

A Map for the Grieving Soul: A Journey Through Psalm 23

PSALM 23 HAS COMFORTED COUNTLESS hearts across the ages, but for those of us who grieve, its words take on a deeper, more personal meaning. It is more than a psalm for funerals or a familiar passage recited in church—it becomes a guide, and a map for the long, difficult journey of loss.

Each verse offers a glimpse of the Shepherd who is both tender and strong. The One who provides for our needs, restores our weary souls, and never leaves our side. He leads us to still waters when rest feels impossible, walks with us through the valley when shadows overwhelm, and protects us with His rod and staff when fear creeps in. He spreads a table for us in our sorrow, anoints us with His Spirit, and fills our lives until they overflow with His grace. And finally, He points us to eternity, where goodness and mercy are our faithful companions and where we will dwell with Him forever.

For the grieving heart, Psalm 23 serves as a God-given roadmap for the soul. It doesn't deny the valleys or erase the shadows, but it shows us that the path runs *through* them, not into them. It teaches us that grief is not the end of our story, but a passage toward healing, restoration, and hope. Along the way, it assures us that the Shepherd never lets go, but that every step we take is accompanied by His presence, His provision, and His promise.

For the grieving heart, Psalm 23 serves as a God-given roadmap for the soul. It teaches us that grief is not the end of our story, but a passage toward healing, restoration, and hope.

Grief has a way of making life feel like a restless storm. The heart aches, the mind races with questions, and peace feels elusive. Yet Psalm 23 reminds us: *"He makes me lie down in green pastures, He leads me beside quiet waters, He restores my soul"* (vv. 2–3). Still waters are not something we must manufacture on our own, they are the gift of the Shepherd who knows our weariness and lovingly guides us to places of rest. These waters may appear in many different forms, but these moments don't erase the grief, but instead restore our strength and remind us that God is still near.

Every grieving soul knows the valley, the place of darkness, fear, and absence. Psalm 23 acknowledges this honestly: *"Even though I walk through the valley of the shadow of death, I will fear no evil, for You are with me"* (v. 4). The promise is not that we will avoid the valley, but that we do not walk it alone. The Shepherd's rod defends us, His staff guides us, and His presence assures us that the shadows cannot destroy us. The valley is real, but so is His nearness. And because He is with us, we are never abandoned in our grief.

In one of the psalm's most surprising images, David writes: *"You prepare a table before me in the presence of my enemies. You anoint my head with oil; my cup overflows"* (v. 5). Even in sorrow, God provides abundance where we expect only emptiness. His Spirit anoints us with comfort, His Word nourishes our souls, and His grace fills us until we overflow. Once again, this abundance doesn't mean the absence of heartache, but it declares that sorrow is not the only reality. God's presence in the valley turns scarcity into abundance, reminding us that His blessings still pursue us, even here, even now.

The psalm concludes with assurance: *"Surely goodness and mercy shall follow me all the days of my life, and I will dwell in the house of the Lord forever"* (v. 6). For those who grieve, this promise is everything. Goodness and mercy are not fleeting, they pursue us daily. And the valley is not our final destination. It's where the Shepherd leads us home.

Psalm 23 is more than ancient poetry. It is a living promise. It tells the truth about grief, but it tells an even greater truth about God: He is with us, He is for us, and He will never leave us. For the grieving soul, it is a map that points us toward hope, guiding us through sorrow and leading us into the eternal presence of the Shepherd who loves us.

CLOSING REFLECTION

The journey of grief is not easy, but Psalm 23 reminds us it is never walked alone. The Shepherd leads, restores, defends, provides, and promises eternal life in His presence. Even in the valley of sorrow, His goodness and mercy pursue us, and His love anchors us. May we carry this truth into our own stories: grief may mark our days, but it does not define them. The Shepherd of our souls does. And one day, He will bring us home.

"The Lord is my shepherd; I shall not want." (Psalm 23:1)

PRAYER FOR THE JOURNEY

Shepherd of our souls, thank you for walking with us through every season of life, through pastures and valleys, through still waters and shadows. Teach us to trust your presence when fear rises, to rest in your care when sorrow overwhelms, and to cling to your promises when hope feels distant. Restore our weary souls with your peace, anoint us with the oil of your Spirit, and let our cups overflow with your grace. Until the day we dwell in your house forever, help us to walk with faith, guided by the assurance that your goodness and mercy are with us always. Amen.

CHAPTER FIFTY

The Story Isn't Over: Hope Beyond the Scars

SCARS ARE STRANGE THINGS. THEY are proof of wounds, yet also proof of healing. Each scar tells us that something once cut us deeply, but it also declares that the wound did not destroy us. In grief, our hearts bear scars no one else can see. These invisible marks are reminders of the love we've lost and the pain we've endured. But as time passes and healing slowly unfolds, our scars begin to speak. They no longer tell a story only of sorrow; they become stories of survival, resilience, and the faithfulness of God.

Looking back, I never imagined I would one day be able to share my story about Melanie without breaking completely. In those first fragile days and months, the pain was raw and all consuming, and I couldn't see past it. But as God gently bound up my broken heart, He began to show me that even my scars had purpose. The wounds that once threatened to undo me became testimonies of His nearness, His strength, and His ability to bring life out of loss.

The world often tells us to hide our scars, to not speak of them and to cover them up as though they are signs of weakness or failure. But in God's Kingdom, scars are holy. As we know, Jesus Himself rose from the grave with scars still visible in His hands and side. When Thomas doubted, Jesus did not hide His scars. Instead,

He invited Thomas to touch them, to see that His suffering was real and that death had not defeated Him. Our Savior's scars became proof of both His pain and His victory.

So, let your scars speak. Let them tell the story of grief and of hope, of sorrow and of survival, of love that endures and faith that refuses to let go.

In much the same way, our scars become part of our witness. When we dare to share our stories of loss and healing, we open the door for others to find comfort and hope. Someone else's valley may feel unbearable until they hear that we, too, have walked through sorrow and survived. Our scars remind them that pain is not the end of the story. They declare that love is stronger than loss, and hope is greater than despair.

Our scars also deepen our compassion. Once we have walked the grief journey, we cannot look at another hurting person the same way. We recognize the weight in their eyes, the ache in their voice, because we've carried it too. Our scars allow us to step into their pain with empathy—not with easy answers but with the assurance that they are not alone. This kind of comfort is powerful because it comes not from theory but from lived experience.

But perhaps most importantly, scars point us forward. They remind us that even though grief leaves a permanent mark, it is not the final word. Just as Jesus' scars told the story of both His suffering and His triumph, so do ours. Every scar says, *"Here is where I was broken, and here is where God met me. Here is where I thought the story was over, and here is where His grace carried me into a new beginning."*

Our scars remind us that death is not the end. The Apostle Paul writes, *"Where, O death, is your victory? Where, O death, is your sting? ... But thanks be to God! He gives us the victory through our Lord Jesus Christ"* (1 Corinthians 15:55, 57). Because of Jesus, the grave has lost its power. His resurrection assures us that those we love who are in Him live on, and that one day, we will be reunited.

So, let your scars speak. Let them tell the story of grief and of hope, of sorrow and of survival, of love that endures and faith that refuses to let go. Let them be reminders that while grief has marked you, it has not defined you. You are not only scarred. You are held, you are loved, and you are being made new.

One day, all our scars will give way to perfect healing. Revelation 21:4 promises, *"He will wipe every tear from their eyes. There will be no more death or mourning or crying or pain, for the old order of things has passed away."* Until that day, let us walk forward with our scars as testimonies, carrying them as proof of God's sustaining grace and of the victory we share in Christ.

Death does not have the final word—Resurrection does! And because of Jesus, our scars will always tell a greater story: a story of love that cannot die, of hope that cannot fade, and of life that will never end.

CLOSING REFLECTION

Our scars are not the end of the story—they are reminders that healing has taken place and that God's grace has carried us through what once felt impossible. Though grief leaves its mark, it also reveals the faithfulness of a Savior who meets us in our pain and brings beauty from the broken places. Every scar becomes a quiet testimony that death is not the final word—Jesus is. And because He lives, our stories continue, marked not by despair, but by enduring hope.

"Those who sow with tears will reap with songs of joy. Those who go out weeping, carrying seed to sow, will return with songs of joy." (Psalm 126:5-6)

PRAYER FOR THE JOURNEY

Lord Jesus, thank you for being the author of our stories, the Redeemer of our scars, and the victor over death. As I carry both love and loss in my heart, teach me to walk with courage and hope. Let my scars reflect your grace, my tears draw me closer to you, and my journey point others to the power of your resurrection. Until the day I see you face to face, and am reunited with those I love, help me to live faithfully, love deeply, and trust fully in your unfailing promises. Amen.

Epilogue

Hᴏᴘᴇ Rᴇᴍᴀɪɴꜱ

As you turn the final pages of this book, my prayer is that you begin to feel less alone in your grief. That through the stories, the prayers, and the promises of Scripture, you've been reminded of the God who sees, who comforts, and who never leaves your side.

Grief may change us, but it does not define us. Love endures, and hope remains. And while sorrow may mark this chapter of our lives, remember, it is not the whole story. The story isn't over. Jesus has the final word, and His word is life.

We live now in the tension of the in between—already held by His peace, but not yet home where every tear will be wiped away. Until that day, we walk forward together, scarred yet strong, broken yet beautiful, carrying both grief and love as testimonies of His faithfulness.

So, take courage, dear one. Keep breathing. Keep walking. Keep trusting that the Shepherd of your soul is still leading you, guiding you, step by small step, until the day He brings you safely home.

PRAYER FOR THE JOURNEY

Lord, thank You for walking with me through the valley of grief. As I step forward into what lies ahead, anchor me in Your love and guide me with Your peace. Remind me that my story, though marked by sorrow, is also marked by hope because of Jesus. May my life reflect Your light until the day I am reunited with those I love and dwell in Your house forever. Amen.

About the Author

PAT ELSBERRY IS AN AUTHOR, speaker, blogger, and Certified Grief Educator whose words bring comfort and hope to hurting hearts. After her daughter, Melanie, ran ahead to Heaven, Pat's life was forever changed. Out of her own grief, she felt a deep calling to walk alongside other parents navigating the unimaginable pain of child loss. Her voice has since become a beacon of compassion and faith, encouraging thousands who are learning to live with loss.

Pat's ministry, Hope During Loss, is rooted in the belief that while grief changes us, God's love sustains us, and even in brokenness, there can be beauty and purpose.

Pat and her family, make their home in Georgia.

You can connect with Pat on a daily basis and follow her speaking schedule.

WWW.HOPEDURINGLOSS.COM
WWW.FACEBOOK.COM/HOPEDURINGLOSS
INSTAGRAM: @HOPEDURINGLOSS

Other Books by Pat Elsberry

Beautifully Broken:
Finding Hope During Loss

Imagine one moment you're heading on vacation and the next moment you're on the phone with a police detective from the Crime Scene Unit.

Then, envision hanging on to the other end of that phone for 90 minutes waiting to find out if the person who was found dead in a hotel room is your child. This is what happened to Pat Elsberry and her family.

Pat's daughter Melanie, died from an accidental drug overdose in February 2020. She was only 38 years old and left behind a lifetime of unfulfilled hopes and dreams. No goodbye. No last hug. Melanie was a beautiful, but broken girl who struggled with the disease of Substance Use Disorder.

Pat invites you to walk through her journey with transparency and vulnerability allowing us to see behind the mask she has always worn. She delivers her story with grit and grace as she tells us how Substance Use Disorder came to be part of her family's life.

AVAILABLE ON AMAZON AND WHEREVER
BOOKS ARE SOLD

Comforted by God
100 Days to Healing and Hope for
the Grief Journey

Pat Elsberry and Boyd Bailey have provided a devotional roadmap pointing the way toward hope, healing, and encouragement for anyone experiencing grief. Having encountered loss and profound grief themselves, the authors offer spiritual insight and practical wisdom to help readers navigate the stages of grief and find their way to strength in God's presence. Whether you are mourning a loss, dealing with trauma, or seeking solace in difficult times, these devotions will be a source of light leading you to the comfort of God.

www.ingramcontent.com/pod-product-compliance
Lightning Source LLC
Chambersburg PA
CBHW060418130626
46555CB00005B/2120